Methods of Mission

Methods of Mission

Edited by

BRIAN R. HOARE

Methodist Publishing House
(for the Home Mission Division of
the Methodist Church)

Methods of Mission

First published by Methodist Publishing House
for the Home Mission Division of the
Methodist Church 1979

7162 0330 8

Made and printed in Great Britain by
Clifford Frost Limited
Wimbledon, London SW19 2SE

Preface

The World Methodist Council's Call to its constituent members to join in intensified mission to the world was made at Denver in 1971 and renewed in Dublin in 1976.

Every one of the 62 Methodist Churches in 90 different countries throughout the world responded positively to the Call and the British Conference in its response urged the Methodist people of Great Britain to prayerful preparation and effective involvement in concentrated mission and evangelism as part of a worldwide witness.

It was acknowledged that many initiatives in mission and evangelism were already being undertaken and it was recognised that mission and evangelism would be variously understood and expressed in the many different situations existing in the churches. No attempt at one stereotyped pattern of activity was suggested or intended and local congregations were urged to determine for themselves what form their outreach should take.

The response to the Call has built up over the years and the launching of the Nationwide Initiative in Evangelism has been a further reminder to churches of all denominations of the importance of evangelism at local level.

It is there that many things are happening and these papers, collected together by the Rev. Brian Hoare, Vice-Chairman of the Conservative Evangelicals in Methodism, have been offered to us as illustrations of just a few of the methods of evangelism that are being used today. We publish them in the hope that they will be of interest and help to churches as they seek to fulfil their missionary opportunities and we shall welcome further examples of evangelistic outreach that can profitably be shared with a wider public.

GEORGE W. SAILS
Chairman, World Methodist
Council Evangelism Committee

Foreword

I am very happy to write a foreword to this set of papers. Almost every part of the Christian Church these days is showing a renewed interest in evangelism. The danger is that our approach to evangelism might be trammelled by our former practices or spoilt by our evangelistic methods dividing us.

In this situation it is necessary that every group within the life of the Church should look again at the basic convictions which dominate its evangelistic concerns, and at the society in which the task of leading people to faith in Christ is to be carried out. In this way we both explore the implications of our traditions and also notice the pressures of change upon us.

In this set of papers, evangelical Methodists are seeking to establish this combination. They are trying to be faithful to genuine evangelical insights into the work of evangelism, while at the same time weighing carefully the pressures upon them of the kind of society in which we live. The authors are themselves regularly engaged in evangelism. They are not simply theorists.

None of the writers would wish, I imagine, to claim finality for what they have written. Rather these are contributions towards a continuing exploration into the ways in which the Good News of Jesus Christ can be made known intelligently and effectively in the modern society in which we live. My hope is that many individuals and groups within the life of the Church will use these papers as a way of stimulating their own thought, and most important of all, as a way of helping them to combine thought about evangelism with engagement in it.

None of us would wish to deny that it is the Holy Spirit who brings men, women and young people to Christ. As we respond to his influence, however, we need to be as clear as possible about the best ways in which we can make ourselves available. My prayer is that these papers will enable many of us to do this, and I am glad to commend them.

DONALD ENGLISH

Contents

Introduction: Some Presuppositions

It was in 1952 that Dr W. E. Sangster first published his little Westminster Pamphlet entitled *Twelve Ways of Evangelism.* It would be presumptuous indeed to imagine that this present publication will have a similar impact, but it does follow a similar pattern. Times have changed in the intervening years and whilst some methods remain unaltered, new ways of spreading the same good news have arisen. Some of these we have sought to describe in these pages.

The chapters which follow make no pretence of being innovatory. Nor do we make any claim that they are an exhaustive list of current evangelistic methods. Much of what we here describe has been done by others before us, and doubtless with equal or even greater effectiveness. Others in our church are engaged in forms of evangelism which find no mention here. We have simply undertaken to collate our experience of using these particular approaches in fulfilling our mission.

It is the hope of all our contributors that what follows will serve both as an 'ideas and resources' document, and as a stimulus to the exploration of yet further ways of spreading the gospel entrusted to us. Some of the contributions will be found to overlap with others, and no attempt has been made to prevent that. Indeed, it is all to the good; for few methods of evangelism are as self-contained as we often like to think of them.

Although we have concentrated on *methods,* we

are not unaware that it is the *message* proclaimed through those methods which is of prior importance. The reader will find here little in the way of theological exploration or theorizing about mission, not because we believe those tasks do not matter but because our purpose lies in another direction. It is all the more important, therefore, that we state briefly what some of our presuppositions have been. We write out of a common allegiance to the evangelical faith, and some of the convictions which undergird the methods we have described may be summarized as follows:

1. We believe evangelism to be a priority for the church.

Dr Sangster ended his *Twelve Ways of Evangelism* with the words 'A church which does not evangelize is hardly a church at all'. He was surely right. Whatever else may or may not be included in our Christian mission to the world, to omit continuous and positive evangelism is to fail the Lord whose last words were 'Go into all the world and preach the gospel to the whole creation'.

2. We believe that true evangelism must include the verbalizing of the gospel.

We may bear witness to that gospel by the life we live; we may show the outworking of that gospel in our Christian service and our social concern; but it is only when we are able to put it into words that men can fully understand what that gospel *is* as well as see what it does. The gospel may well be implicit in all our church activities, but our work does not become true evangelism until we make our message explicit by a clear proclamation of the faith by which we live. To do less than that is to offer men the fruit while denying them the root.

3. We believe the heart of the evangelistic message to be 'Jesus Christ and him crucified'.

We are not concerned merely to fill our pews. We are not seeking primarily to get people to adopt Christian standards. We are not in business to commend or defend the church. We seek, like Mr Wesley, to 'offer Christ' — to introduce men to Jesus. But it is 'Christ *crucified*' we preach. There is power only in a gospel with a cross at the centre of it and a Risen Christ as the theme of it. Our message is summed up in a Person: 'Jesus our Lord, who was put to death for our trespasses and raised for our justification' (Romans 4:25). We offer him to men not merely as a pattern of life to be copied, but as a living saviour to be received and served.

4. We believe in the absolute necessity of conversion.

It is not an experience that 'keen' Christians may have, but that others may do without. All our methods of mission are aimed at bringing men to a conscious and personal decision to turn from the old life and to give themselves wholly to Christ. A man may be a churchgoer, a church member or even a church leader, but only when he deliberately opens his life to the lordship of Christ can he rightly be called 'Christian'.

It is convictions such as these, then, which have spurred us on to explore the methods of mission described in these pages. But methods alone can save no man. It is the gospel itself which is 'the power of God for salvation to everyone who has faith' (Romans 1:16). It may be that these methods are not your methods. So be it. What is beyond doubt, however, is that it is incumbent upon us all by *some* method to offer our fellow men the truth as it is in Jesus.

1 Mission in the City

GEOFFREY L. CLARK

*Minister of Brunswick Methodist Church,
Newcastle-upon-Tyne*

The reality of the modern city with its commercial centre, inner belt, large housing estates and suburbs, is too important to ignore in our evangelism. Some may claim that the only difference between the village and the city is one of scale, but they fly in the face of the evidence. The size, structures and style of urban living all combine to make it different and in turn to affect the lives of city dwellers. The noise, speed and stress of living; the cheek to cheek existence of deprivation and abundance; the power of the institutions to bring affluence or redundancy to thousands; the ever-expanding sophisticated care and declining neighbourliness alike mark modern urban society.

In the city man becomes dependent on others, not so much on the individual but on the organised community. At the time of writing, for instance, Local Authority workers are on strike, so that my children are home from school, refuse forms mountains behind the city stores and all but the emergency cases wait in vain for an ambulance to take them to hospital. The city is big and busy, exhilarating and depressing, a place of hope and a place of despair . . .

. . . and in the city lives the church, worshipping and serving, its buildings standing as a reminder of its permanence, often speaking with louder voices than its people, declaring an allegiance to days long past so that stepping from the modern home through its solid doors is like stepping into a distant age. We forget the importance of the attractive entrance and the open door, yet a walk through the shopping streets of any modern city should be sufficient to remind us.

Modern cities are all different, but they have in common one experience: change. We accept it, yet at the same time it is resented. The demolition men removing old landmarks also shake our foundations as they nibble at symbols of our security. I referred to this once when serving as visiting lecturer at an Anglican community's ecumenical week; but an elderly gentleman, whose patent sanctity was a blessing to us all, could not bear to think that it should affect the church. 'Sir', he blurted out, 'the church must not change. It is that which remains constant in our society!' I knew what he meant, indeed I longed to agree with him, but in truth I could not. For whilst the Lord of the church remains the same, his Body changes as it responds to those around it. Its response is both in its service and in its evangelism, which must begin with listening to the call of the city.

It is unthinkable that Jesus should not have listened to the call of Bartimaeus, or to the voice of need rising from a hungry multitude; or that having listened he should have said 'No, your problem is something else; I will deal with that'. Often, indeed, men's recognised needs were but symptoms of a deeper need, but Jesus never ignored them. He saw their need, heard their voice and responded to them in love.

The church must follow him. It will read the signs

of the times using the insights into the nature of the city which the sociologists and others make available, learning about movement and change in urban society and, in applying its mind to these things, growing in understanding of the world in which God has set it down. A foundation statement of any church must be: 'God has set us down in *this* place. How do we serve him *here?*' In the city we forget this at our peril. A city church which bears no relevance to the city's needs will not last long.

The church's work is both to make Christians and to build them up. These are not separate tasks; there is no either/or choice here, for both are vital and the church's evangelism will only be effective when it is doing them both. How is all this to be achieved?

I do not devote space here to state the importance of preaching and of personal witness. That is not because I do not value them, but rather because they must be assumed as always being basic to the church's witness. Many others could give illustrations of effective evangelism in the city; I offer just two stories.

The first is of a regional event. It was a Christian festival entitled 'Celebrate the Faith'. From the earliest planning stages it was seen to be in two parts: a City Hall event with nightly meetings attended by a crowd of well over two thousand and addressed by a well-known Anglican minister possessed of remarkable gifts as a teacher and evangelist; and in other places in the city centre, forums, discussions, music, drama and open-air events each speaking about the love of God and the presence of Christ in the modern city. There was clear affirmation of Christ as Lord and Saviour, and through the festival Christians were made and built up.

It all began in a most remarkable way, for at one and the same time, and without any prior consultation, the Council of Evangelical Churches and a local Council of Churches began to explore the possibility of a mission to the city. There were obvious theological differences. These were not blinked at, but neither were they permitted to stop co-operation. The result was that groups as far apart as the Brethren and the Roman Catholics were able to play their part in it.

Preparation was made both in the committee room and in the prayer room. Not only were individuals, groups and churches asked to pray for the event, but special Bible study and preparation courses, generally on a common theme, were arranged in the churches around the city. Frequently the groups were ecumenical.

Throughout the festival one was aware that the vast majority of those attending were Christians who came in by the car and coach load. Nevertheless the effect of the large gatherings was to inspire, encourage, challenge and teach. The smaller events made a Christian response to the problems of the region including unemployment, housing and homelessness and press responsibility. They included celebrations in music, drama and dance, as well as in worship and sacrament, and through these the word and healing of Christ were offered.

The second story is of a neighbourhood church engaged in evangelism in its immediate area. Here the method differed. A long-term programme was prepared and a strategy developed which included a period devoted to getting to know the neighbourhood and its people. This meant visiting in a systematic manner, not with the intention of saying 'We are from the church; come and join us', but rather in order to discover first what people were thinking and to find out about their needs. The next stage was in responding to those needs through befriending, through the creation of caring groups, through the offer of teaching and fellowship in situations where the faith could be freely discussed, and through special services which clearly declared the eternal truths of the gospel. The result of all this was that the church became a centre in the neighbourhood where people knew that help was to be found, and where lives were seen to be being changed. It was marked by its open door, its love and the clear Christian statement of why it existed.

*   *   *

From these two stories there are lessons to be learned:
1. Evangelism is most effective when it shows that Jesus came to meet people where they are. The declaration of Christian truth has to be accompanied by taking the fruit of that truth to the people in the neighbourhood which the church serves. There are many ways in which the city church can be seen to be interested in and concerned for the life of the city, not least by making its premises available for all manner of societies and organisations to use during the week.
2. Evangelism must start with an understanding of people, and must include a response to their needs. It will therefore need to be closely linked with a programme of care. A Baptist church in a part of the city conspicuous for bad housing and social problems has found that its mission has led it to

engage in action for improving the standards of the area in co-operation with the local Community Association. Its evangelical traditions were well-known, but it had to show that the gospel was good news for those in poor housing and others at the bottom of the social pile. This is but one way. Other churches have experimented by seeking to provide day-time club facilities for the unemployed school-leavers of the area. In yet another the Probation Service, Youth for Christ and a city church arrange special activities for youngsters in trouble, offering them 'abundant life' physically, mentally and spiritually. The possibilities are many, and will depend on the particular needs of the community which the church serves. Always, however, the response will be costly; and always there is the important task of making it clear that what is being offered is not mere humanitarian help but an expression of the gospel.

3. Evangelism is most effective when programmed into the ongoing life of the church, and not slipped in like an occasional injection. We think of it too often as a kind of 'snatch squad' operation, the Christian soldier making the occasional foray into a dangerous world to snatch someone from the enemy and bring him into the safety of the fortress church. Rather, everything, every organisation, every activity needs to be geared as part of the church's evangelistic ministry. Sometimes that will mean starting new activities. The Methodist Mission in one city became troubled about the many lonely elderly people in its area, and in co-operation with the local branch of Age Concern furnished a comfortable lounge and called it the 'Pop In' centre.

Now hundreds of elderly citizens pop in each week, and a regular ministry to them has been established. A city centre church in Lancashire which is used daily by one secular group or another has furnished an attractive lounge area in its entrance hall and set up a stand of bright Christian literature for people to sit and browse through or buy. In other city centre situations it has proved possible to run weekly Lunch Hour Talks to cater for workers in shops and offices who enjoy a change of venue while they eat their sandwiches, and such activities have proved quite fruitful.

4. Evangelism needs to be in co-operation with Christians of other denominations wherever this is possible. In Hull, for instance, the city centre ministers' fraternal took the initiative in promoting monthly evangelical rallies under the local ecumenical banner 'Link Up'. In another city the lesson of co-operation is seen in ventures in caring for vagrants in which Roman Catholic sisters share with a group of evangelical laymen. Such work does not deny the differences, but recognizes that Christ is bigger than they are.

For further thought and action

Among the helpful books dealing with the problems faced by the church in city areas are:

Sheppard, David, *Built as a City* (Hodder)

Benington, John, *Culture, Class and Christian Beliefs* (Scripture Union).

A helpful pack of material designed to enable the city church to analyse both itself and its neighbourhood is available from:

URBAN CHURCH PROJECT, St Matthias Vicarage, Poplar High Street, London E14 04E.

2 Mission in Rural Areas

HAROLD A. ANFIELD

Superintendent Minister of the Sherburn Circuit in North Yorkshire

The preacher peered through the gloomy haze created by the stove whose ill-fitting chimney seemed to release as much smoke inside the chapel as it did outside. His congregation of two elderly ladies settled down for worship. Both lived in neighbouring villages. Sometimes they were joined by between two and four members of a family from yet another village. It was all in an attempt to keep alive the witness in the village in which the chapel was situated, and from which not a single person came to share in worship. One could hardly feel surprised at this indifference. The chapel premises showed all too clearly the signs of serious neglect. Set back from the side road the entrance could only be reached by walking through knee-deep grass, and once through the door one was greeted with soot and dust! It is true that one of the ladies brought a duster with her each Sunday to wipe the six places that might be used, though she never seemed to remember the pulpit! It is astonishing what conditions the faithful, whether in town or country, are sometimes prepared to accept, and also how insensitive they can often be to the extremely poor impression they are conveying to the people round about whom presumably they hope to influence and win for Christ and his church.

It was felt in the Circuit generally that the days of

this little chapel must surely be numbered. Some were already suggesting that it should be closed. Many of the villagers, as we were to discover in the course of a house-to-house visitation, thought that it was unused. "You'll close it over my dead body", was the reaction of the elder of the two ladies who regularly attended the services, and who for years had been the Society Steward. She commanded wide respect as a woman of deep loyalty and devotion, and undoubtedly prevented the threatened closure.

Then, one morning, a tradesman called at her cottage home. She was sitting beside her unlit fire, but her soul was with God. The chapel overflowed with the crowd that attended her funeral service, which was an occasion of triumph and joy. The local vicar was present to pay his respects. What now, though, was to happen to the chapel she had so stoutly defended? It would certainly be easier to facilitate its closure, but no one was prepared to propose this. In the Circuit Meeting the feeling was expressed that some effort should be made to revive the cause. Almost surprisingly this gained unanimous support, though we were to become very much aware that the Holy Spirit was directing what was to happen. It was decided to invite Cliff College to send two evangelists to conduct a mission in the village.

Enthusiasm for this venture grew rapidly. There was the problem of the very poor condition of the premises. This was tackled by the young people of the Circuit. They moved in with scythes, mops and paintbrushes, and soon began to transform the scene. The troublesome stove was removed, and a Steward of another Society in the Circuit donated four storage heaters. Meanwhile, prayer was intensified that all the

9

work of preparation might be under the leading of the Holy Spirit, and that the mission might prove to be very fruitful.

So the villagers became aware that the chapel was still in business after all. The vicar was advised of what was happening, and co-operated helpfully in numerous ways. Door-to-door visitation was so planned as to ensure three visits to each home prior to the commencement of the meetings. One very successful result of this part of the preparation was the establishing of a Sunday School. A mother expressed, across her doorstep, disappointment that there was no Sunday School in the village to which she and her sister could send their children. The visitor discovered that between them they had ten children, and promised to see what could be done for them. They were to form the basis of a School that commenced immediately at the conclusion of the special meetings. Another discovery was that most of the people who expressed interest in the Sunday Service much preferred one to be held in the morning rather than the evening. As a result of this the Service time was altered from 6.00 p.m. to 11.00 a.m.

When the evangelists arrived they found the ground prepared and the people expectant. For ten days they visited, preached and counselled. Thanks to the support that the Circuit gave, the chapel was full night by night so no casual visitor felt isolated or conspicuous with a pew to himself. Meetings were held in the early evening for children, and were followed by the meetings for adults. Numerous conversions were recorded, and much blessing came both to the village and to the wider Circuit. There was also a bonus for one of the evangelists! During the mission he heard clearly the call of God to the ministry, and has since been ordained as a Methodist minister.

After the special meetings the fruits of the children's work were gathered up in the newly commenced Sunday School, which was staffed by two volunteer teachers from another village. Congregations improved to about ten adults. With an average of eighteen children attending, this meant that there were almost thirty souls praising and serving the Lord in a little chapel that had seemed to be doomed. It is still, of course, a very small cause, but its doors remain open to welcome in the name of the Lord all who will pass through them. I think I see the familiar smile on the face of that valiant soul now in glory, and hear her glad shout — 'Hallelujah'!

*   *   *

Arising out of this story (which took place in the Droxford Circuit in Hampshire) and subsequent experience in rural Circuits elsewhere, the following observations may be made:

1. God is speaking to us in the difficult situations facing our rural churches today. We need to be aware of the danger of being so preoccupied with our own ideas and solutions that we fail to hear what he is saying. All our planning and endeavour needs to be prayerfully determined under the direction, and with the enabling, of the Holy Spirit. Even seemingly 'hopeless causes' can be renewed if we discern and follow his way.

2. The Circuit is perhaps a more important unit in rural areas than it is for more self-sufficient urban churches. A Circuit Conference, called for the

11

purposes of considering the work of God amongst us, and open to all who care to come, can be a useful means of evaluating what is being done and of seeking the Spirit's guidance for the future. If a Circuit is willing to provide the resources of money and manpower for evangelistic endeavour in selected villages, small causes that might otherwise die through their ability to help themselves can be revitalised. Much can be accomplished at a Circuit or sectional level which could never be attempted by one village church alone. For instance, a rural Circuit in Derbyshire attracts some 80-100 young people to a Circuit Youth Ramble followed by a young peoples' service two or three times a year, yet only a couple of the churches in the Circuit has its own YPF group! In my present Circuit we run a regular evangelistic rally which is well supported from the Circuit and beyond, but which few, if any, of the individual churches would be able to hold on its own.

3. The goodwill and co-operation of neighbouring churches should be cultivated wherever possible. In most rural situations this means the Parish Church. It is a courtesy to advise the vicar of special evangelistic plans. He will usually appreciate such a gesture, whether or not he feels able to support what we are doing. If Anglican support is forthcoming, so much the better. Regular co-operation between 'church' and 'chapel' can be a very effective means of evangelism in country areas. United Family Services tend to attract some villagers occasionally who do not attend otherwise, particularly when children are involved. Some villages now have a united Anglican-Methodist Sunday School, to the

mutual benefit of both churches and, not least, to the village. Weekday activities can sometimes be usefully combined also. Some country Methodists are happier identifying themselves with united inter-denominational activities in their own village than with united Methodist activities in some distant town or village.

4. Rural churches, perhaps more conservative than their urban counterparts, need to be willing to adjust to modern situations. Take, for example, the timing of our Sunday services. It is clear that those held in the morning are the best attended of the day in the majority of cases. Many country Methodists, however, have their one service of the day in the afternoon — the most unpopular time of all in my experience. Many more walk through unlit or dimly lit roads and lanes to attend their one service of the week when the sun has set. Can we really wonder that our numbers are so small?

5. Our buildings need to be as clean, comfortable and warm as we can make them inside, and as well-kept as possible outside. Few people are likely to be attracted into a building that looks run-down and dowdy, however attractive the activity going on inside. Where our facilities are adequate (a school-room and kitchen) it is all to the good to have them used by other village organisations (Young Farmers Club, WI, Darby and Joan, Playgroup, Parish Council) so that the chapel is seen as an integral part of village life.

6. Children's work needs to be maintained at all costs, both for the sake of the children and also because of the invaluable link it provides with their parents and families. Nor are some of the more ambitious

13

children's activities out of reach for the village church where even a handful of workers are prepared to make some sacrifice. A 'Children's Holiday Club' held during the summer some years ago in the village of Hunmanby, North Yorkshire, attracted up to seventy children, was voted by many parents 'the best thing that's happened for years', led to a crowded follow-up meeting in the autumn at which slides of the Holiday Club were shown, boosted the regular Sunday School attendance considerably and brought at least a couple of children into the life of the church who have remained into their teenage years.

None of what is written here will provide a blueprint for guaranteed success in rural mission, but attention prayerfully given to these things may well lead under God to a regaining of confidence and a renewal of vision in some of our country churches. There are many signs of hope to encourage us today. The divine commission to go and make disciples has not been withdrawn; neither has the promise of our risen Saviour to abide continually with those who obey and, in the power of the Spirit, to make them his witnesses.

Some useful addresses

DATCHET EVANGELICAL FELLOWSHIP, Datchet House, Church Lane, Whitton, Ipswich, Suffolk IP1 6TJ.

A society involved in re-establishing and maintaining a permanent evangelical witness in rural areas (mainly East Anglia).

FELLOWSHIP FOR EVANGELISING BRITAIN'S VILLAGES, Little Tey Road, Feering, Colchester, Essex CO5 9RN.

A society engaged in village evangelism among both adults and children throughout the UK.

MISSION FOR CHRIST, 48 Havelock Road, Hastings, East Sussex TN34 1BE

A society seeking to train and supply a variety of evangelistic and pastoral ministries for rural Britain nationwide.

SUMMER CRUSADES, Wentworth House, Aldbrough, Nr Hull, North Humberside.

A mission running campaigns and village treks for both adults and children (particularly in the North of England).

Some useful publications

Clarke, John E., *Mission in Rural Communities* (Home Mission Division).

Country Pattern (Home Mission Occasional Paper).

Youth and the Rural Church (Home Mission Occasional Paper).

Luke, H., *Mission to the Rural Community* (Luton Industrial College).

Luke, H., *The Church in the Rural Community* (Luton Industrial College).

A Workbook on Rural Evangelism (ACE Diocesan House, Quarry Street, Guildford, Surrey)

3 Children's Missions and Holiday Bible Clubs

D AVID S AVAGE

Methodist Local Preacher working as a Children's Evangelist on the staff of Scripture Union

Most churches are already engaged in some form of outreach amongst young people through the Sunday School, Junior Church, Youth Club, Bible Class and the various uniformed organisations. Although this regular pattern of Christian education is already established, however, an increasing number of churches are discovering the value of occasional special children's events such as a mission or holiday club, planned as an activity of the whole church in order to supplement and support the regular work amongst the children. The children's mission provides for more concentrated teaching of Bible stories and Christian truths, presented in a lively and relevant manner, and gives the opportunity for response to those truths as appropriate. It is not only an occasion for challenging those children who have been faithfully taught through the regular activities, however, but often also enables the church to reach children and their families who have previously had little contact with the local church.

The results of a children's mission go far beyond the number of young people who, in their own way, make their decision to follow Christ. The mission has far reaching effects in the community. The following list summarises some of the comments that have been made by church leaders describing the benefits of a children's mission in their church:

1. Numbers in the Sunday School/Junior Church increased.
2. Interest in regular Bible reading was greatly stimulated.
3. Some 'lapsed' children returned and there was a renewed eagerness and enthusiasm for Sunday School.
4. There were closer relationships between teachers and children.
5. Sunday School teachers and helpers were challenged to a deeper commitment themselves.
6. An increased fellowship and sense of purpose was generated through the teachers working closely together during the mission.
7. There was a greater awareness of the needs of young people and of their leaders among the main body of church members.
8. Enormous goodwill was generated in the community served by the church.
9. Good contact was made with parents and they were challenged themselves concerning faith in Christ.

The programme options for a children's mission are manifold, and largely determined by the overall aims. The most popular alternatives have been found to be those described below.

Term-time missions

Meetings can be held after school or in the early evening each night for a week or more, the series perhaps beginning or ending (or both) with a Family Service, and including some other family event during the week. It is usual to hold separate meetings for each age group, as it is difficult to meet the needs of too wide an age spread in one session. The following is one way to divide the age groups:

Infants	(5-7 years) before tea	4.00-4.45pm
Juniors	(7-11 years) after tea	6.00-7.30pm
Inters	(11-13 years) early evening	7.45-8.45pm

It is best to give the Juniors a break between school and the meeting, as this ensures that parents know where the children are, results in a better atmosphere, and gives them a chance to let off steam before they come!

The advantages of this type of term-time mission are considerable. All the children are available, none being away on holiday, and the church's youth programme is already in full swing thus allowing for good follow on. Further contact can be made with the children through any day school visits it is possible to arrange, and evening meetings allow those Sunday School teachers who work during the day to participate in the mission. A mission of this sort provides opportunity for good continuity of concentrated teaching, and often has the added advantage that mothers may attend the meetings for the Infants age group and learn much themselves from what is being taught to their children.

It must be recognised that a term-time mission may run into difficulties by clashing with children's other regular non-church commitments (Brownies, Swimming Club and so on), and it may be that dark, wet winter evenings will discourage children whose parents are not prepared to provide transport. Again, some Sunday School teachers may be unable to share in the earlier meetings, or may have other regular commitments that make attendance every night impossible.

It has been found best to avoid the first and last weeks of term and to miss December altogether for this type of mission. The most fruitful times seem to be September or early October when the youth programme is starting up again after the summer break, or the period from late March to early June (avoiding Easter which may affect follow on work).

An extended term-time series

This is a variation of the term-time mission consisting of a series of meetings held on the same evening each week for a 4-6 week period. It is particularly appropriate for Juniors and Inters, and is ideal when the follow-on is to take the form of a mid-week Bible Club. Although it does not have the advantage of enabling the same amount of concentrated teaching as a week-long mission, and it may not have the same appeal for children not already in the Sunday School, it does have other compensating advantages. An evening can be chosen which avoids clashes with other activities, pressure on the helpers is reduced, and it eases homework problems for the 11-13s. Parents too are more likely to turn out to bring their children for one night a week rather than five on the trot.

Holiday Clubs

Like the term-time mission, Holiday Clubs consist of a week of special meetings, but this time held during the school holidays and run during the daytime. Meetings for Infants and Juniors are normally held in the mornings and may include a joint worship session with plenty of lively songs and choruses. Teaching and other activities will be in age-groups, and sometimes the programme may be extended into the afternoon with games and other activities. Meetings for Inters are usually best held separately in the late afternoon or early evening.

The Holiday Club has many advantages. The extra time available makes possible a greater variety of activities, and the main worship and teaching programme can be supplemented by more group activity with just six or eight children attached to one helper to work together on an activity leaflet with puzzles and projects based on the day's teaching. Models, craftwork and games are all possible. These small groups are immensely valuable and build deep relationships between adult Christians and children as they get alongside them and get to know the members of their group as individuals. If it is true that faith is caught rather than taught, then group time is highly infectious! An added advantage of the Holiday Club is the possibility of increased parental involvement. Some mums may be glad to help by preparing drinks and biscuits for a mid-morning break, and dads could be roped in to help with afternoon games. One Methodist Holiday Club in the North of England organised a sports day for the final Saturday which involved a large number of parents in a variety of different capacities.

One obvious disadvantage of the Holiday Club is that some children are bound to be away on holiday. It will demand more from helpers in both time and effort, and more extensive premises will be needed for the additional activites. Follow-on may be hampered by holidays, although some churches have found a 'reunion' at the beginning of the autumn term has helped here.

*   *   *

Having described the various types of children's mission we must go on to consider some other important questions about them.

Leader and Team

The mission leader will have overall responsibility for the programme, and will normally lead the main sessions himself. He must be able to relate to children well, communicate effectively with them and control them in an informal situation. He must command the respect of the helpers and be able to direct them and delegate them. He has the task of training them, and co-ordinating the whole programme.

It is sometimes an advantage to import a leader from outside, and he will often bring fresh insights, experience and ideas. Scripture Union children's evangelists (four of whom, incidentally, were trained at Cliff College) are always glad to help here, and are being increasingly used in Methodist churches. But it is by no means essential to use a 'professional' leader. A local leader has the advantage of knowing the children already, and of a continuing relationship with them once the mission is over. The Sunday School superintendent may, or may not, have the gifts required for leading the mission, and it need not be assumed that he must act as leader. The job could be given to a member of the church who, for one reason or another, is not involved regularly in the Sunday School but has the necessary gifts for this special event.

However good the leader, he will need plenty of help! Children need to be welcomed as they arrive, there are names and addresses to record, 'subs' to collect, groups to be led, activities to be supervised. The bookstall will need to be manned, and at the close there must be careful supervision at the door, with possibly a road-crossing patrol outside. I have tried to aim at the following number of children per adult helper:

	Term-time mission	Holiday Club
Infants	10	5
Juniors	15	8
Inters	10	10

It is possible, of course, to import a team (students from a local Meth. Soc. or Christian Union may be glad to help), but it is far better to use members of the local church. There are many who, whilst they cannot commit themselves to regular Sunday School work, would be glad to help for the duration of a mission. To involve local church members beyond the Sunday School staff will enrich both the mission and the church. It will strengthen the children's work through the training and experience the mission brings, and avoids the vacuum that sometimes accompanies the departure of a visiting team.

Preparation and follow-up

Someone has said 'You should plan as if everything depended on you, and pray as if everything depended on God'. The whole church needs to be mobilised to support the mission in prayer as soon as the first plans are laid. Members can be kept informed of progress through a church news sheet. Each team member could undertake to pray regularly for a small number of children and their families.

Mission planning must be realistic. The greatest temptations are either not to be ambitious enough or to attempt too much and thus overstretch the resources available. It is better to do one thing at a time and do it well, than to aim at a lot and hit nothing!

Every session will need detailed planning. The mission leader will normally be responsible for the choice of Biblical material to be used, and once a theme for the week has been chosen then other activities, quizzes, games, expression work, audio-visual aids and serial stories can be arranged around it to make for as much variety, excitement and interest as possible. Other helpers will need to be trained to share in the talks, lead the singing and short prayers, quizzes and memory work, and it is important that helpers are also adequately trained to help children who may wish to know more about the Christian life.

The follow-up to the mission needs to be planned along with the actual programme. All new contacts will need visiting personally with a view to integrating them into the ongoing life of the church. New ideas will need to be incorporated into the regular weekly programme, and a Bible reading group or junior youth fellowship may need to be established for those who are really in earnest about following Christ. Parents, too, will need following up after the mission, and possibly monthly informal meetings for parents and children (Harvest Supper, games night, bonfire night, carol service) will pave the way for attendance at Family Worship. It has often been found useful to have at least one meeting for families during the actual mission week itself, usually on the Friday or Saturday. To have the children taking part is a good way of getting the parents along, for their appetite is already whetted by what they have heard from the children during the week. Parents have been known to be converted through such meetings as these!

The financing of the mission will need facing early on. If a leader and team from outside are being used they will need to be given reasonable expenses. Craft materials, paint and glue, activity leaflets and publicity materials all cost money, and whilst at a Holiday Club it is possible to levy a small charge from the children, it is probably better for the church to undertake the financing of the mission itself.

Careful use of publicity material can both ensure support and control the number and type of children attending. Let it be determined by your aims for the week. Sunday School children and their friends can simply be given an attractively printed folder or card together with a letter to their parents, but if the aim is to reach as many children as possible further publicity can often be given through local school assemblies and a widespread poster campaign. But beware! Big is not beautiful in children's work. Adults may like to be lost in a crowd, but children don't. A mass invasion from the area will achieve little and may even frighten away some of your own Sunday School children. Keep well within your resources, therefore, and remember that if there are more than a hundred or so children the leader will not have spoken to them all individually before the week is out. A big crowd may be impressive but it is far better to make real progress with a few than to be inundated with children for a week only to find that no deep and lasting work has been achieved.

For further information

Gordon Pettie *How to have a Holiday Club* (Scripture Union).

A practical and helpful addition to SU's list of *Know How Books.*

Some useful addresses

The Missions Secretary, SCRIPTURE UNION, PO Box 38, Bristol BS9 9NA (Telephone: Bristol 771131).

He will be glad to put you in touch with the SU staff worker in your area who is available either to give advice and training for those leading a mission themselves, or to prepare and lead a mission or Holiday Club for you.

CHRISTIAN PUBLICITY ORGANISATION, Ivy Arch Road, Worthing, Sussex.

CPO provide an attractive range of pre-printed cards, leaflets and posters at very reasonable rates. Samples will be sent on request.

SOUND AND VISION UNIT, Scripture Union, 47 Marylebone Lane, London W1M 6AX.

Suppliers of a wide range of soundstrips, tapes and discussion starters for children's work. Send for a catalogue.

4 Evangelism in a Pop Culture

ROB FROST

Minister in the London Mission (Tooting) Circuit

This is the age of the media. We are surrounded by 'musical wallpaper', conditioned by advertising gimmicks, and entertained by the world of *Crossroads* and *Emmerdale Farm.* This 'pop' culture is a far cry from the era of the gospel rally, the travelling preacher and the evangelistic tract.

Some years ago some friends and I dreamt up what we thought was a fantastic idea. We invited folk to a village rally by erecting a twelve foot long day-glow poster outside the chapel. The poster became a talking point . . . but only the regulars turned up for the rally! We needed to learn what television chief Sir Charles Curran described as 'an ability to convince the audience of their own wish to expose themselves to what we want to say.' The modern evangelist must learn how to catch and hold the audience's attention.

The use of modern media in evangelism is not religious entertainment or 'compromise with the world'; it is simply effective communication. The modern media do not change or cheapen the gospel. They do not replace preaching, but complement it. The language of film, music, drama and dance is the vernacular of the new generation, and we must learn to speak it. What follows is not an exhaustive survey, but simply a few methods that I have found effective in proclaiming Christ today.

Street Theatre

My first fumbling attempts at 'street theatre' were on Blackpool beach in July 1970. Our Cliff College trek team was finding great difficulty in gathering a crowd for its open air meeting. No matter how eloquent our material or how fervently we shouted, the people walked by pretending not to notice! It was an embarrassing experience for us and our hearers.

One day, however, we introduced a whole range of dramatic 'characters' into the proceedings. Different team members dressed up as the 'absent minded professor', the 'football hooligan', the 'businessman in a hurry', and the 'materialistic mechanic'. The arrival of these strangely dressed actors brought the people flocking round, and the interviews with each character produced laughter and applause. Our message was inherent in the dialogue; we were getting through at last.

Street theatre is a simple but effective means of communication and I have seen it work in lots of different situations. Hundreds heard the story of Jesus and the paralytic as they gathered to watch four robed men lower a stretcher to the beach. Hordes of children followed Goliath along the promenade to watch his confrontation with young David. Amazing applause followed a presentation of Jonah during a swimming break in an open air pool. A large covered shopping centre was the setting for the prodigal son story; and a traffic free city street proved a good site for the parable of the rich fool.

Our teams have always consulted the police about suitable sites, and we have generally found them most helpful. We have usually looked for a traffic-free area with a large flow of pedestrians, and we have ruled out the use of amplification, as it can become a public nuisance. Whilst the link man has told the story and made the application, the three or four actors in colourful costume have drawn the crowd. About a dozen other team members have mingled with the people, distributing literature and taking up opportunities for conversation. Enquirers have been taken back to a church hall for coffee. Street theatre has been primarily a seed-sowing ministry; but there have been conversions through the personal witness among the crowd.

Films

There has been a remarkable recovery in the British cinema over recent years, and box office winners like *Star Wars* and *Superman* have brought capacity audiences to many film centres. Besides being a favourite form of entertainment, film is also a very powerful communicator.

Several new Christian film libraries have appeared in recent years; but there are still very few religious films that I can recommend for outreach activities. The cost of producing such films must be colossal; and I have found that a 'superstar' name on the publicity is essential to draw in a non-Christian audience. Currently I am using *The Cross and the Switchblade* starring Pat Boone, *Gospel Road* with Johnny Cash, and the slightly dated film *Two a Penny* featuring Cliff Richard. An excellent 'short' to run before these main features is *The Cobbler,* a brilliant animation of Tolstoy's classic story. A new release, *No Longer Alone,* starring James Fox and Simon Williams looks a promising addition to the list.

One summer afternoon we distributed two thousand glossy handouts advertising the film *Two a*

Penny to holidaymakers in Newquay, Cornwall. Over a hundred of them turned up for the evening show; and a repeat of the experiment over the next three weeks brought the same result. Tickets were sold for each performance, and the provision of free coffee after the film encouraged people to stay behind and talk. Many holidaymakers completed follow-up cards asking for further information about the Christian faith. Similar experiments in towns, villages and cities have been equally effective.

I have generally used two projectors and four speakers when showing a main feature film. Obviously adequate blackout, a good screen and comfortable seating have been important. I have avoided beginning such meetings with a hymn or prayer because people have come to watch, not worship. A very brief address has sometimes been appropriate after the film; but I have always spoken using the film as my basis. A full-blown gospel sermon has never seemed suitable. The most fruitful part of the evening has often been the conversation over coffee afterwards, and I have known folk find Christ at the end of film evenings such as these.

Music

Gospel music has come a long way since we used to dim the lights in the church cellar and ask one of the youth group to sing *Kumbaya*! Sadly, many churches haven't kept up. The gospel music concert is a very effective method of communicating Christ to those who follow different styles of music. Christian musicians in the country and western, new wave, rock or folk idiom can make a powerful witness by the lyrics they sing and their comments between songs.

Our youth group decided to try to reach their peer

group around town. New wave music was the idiom that most of their friends were involved in, so the Bill Mason Band was deemed the most suitable Christian group. Realising that most of their friends would never be seen dead in a church, they booked the local Comprehensive School hall for the evening. Older churchgoers would probably have been shocked by the loud and raucous music and the way that the group leapt about the stage with amazing agility. Yet by the end of the concert the 150 teenagers present were in no doubt as to what the Gospel was, and how they should respond to it.

In order to communicate to the difficult 18-30 group in our town we booked the close harmony group Nutshell for an evening concert. Glossy publicity and expensive tickets brought in nearly 200 young people to hear a highly professional selection of gospel music punctuated by testimony. This group cost £150 plus expenses, but the costs were recouped by the sale of tickets. The impact on the rather more sophisticated young person who felt that church was 'old hat' was definite.

A team of witnessing Christians at such concerts has always been effective. They have mingled with the crowd during the interval and after the concert. The provision of a paperback bookstall and free literature has also been worth while.

Gospel Roadshow

I was full of apprehension when we embarked on our first 'Gospel Roadshow' in July 1975. To say the least, it was something of an experiment. Touring from London to York to Plymouth with a van load of equipment and a double-decker full of young people was certainly an experience! We did make an awful lot of mistakes, but the concept of a travelling roadshow was right. It was a fruitful mission, and night after night we found youngsters eager to hear more about Jesus Christ.

Over the years we have developed a programme suitable for a wide age-range and have presented roadshows in myriad situations including theatres in the United States, bars in Spain, and schools and churches in Britain. The basis is simple. Gather together a group of committed Christians talented in music, drama, dance and comedy . . . and develop a programme of witness and testimony.

The roadshows have been exhausting and demanding work, yet more than any other kind of evangelism in which I have been involved in recent years they have been a bridge of communication between the church and the world. We have used roadshows as effective Circuit Rallies, and for reaching the uncommitted on the Community Roll. Many folk have found Christ through the presentation of the gospel in this way.

Mass Media

Many Christians have failed to see the evangelistic possibilities within newspapers, radio and television. Often these areas are seen as the domain of the professionals, and although a basic ability to communicate is essential many suitable writers have just not tried. A few examples of how to penetrate this area might be helpful.

A local hospital administrator arranged for us to have a weekly slot on hospital radio. Every Sunday lunchtime in a studio about the size of a wardrobe we broadcast music and testimony to a number of London hospitals.

The submission of some trial articles to a small Yorkshire weekly paper led to the allocation of a weekly column called *Frost on Friday*. The response to this small weekly message was amazing. One day I even met a young couple who had been blessed by the column when they received the paper in South Africa!

Newsmen are always looking for local human interest, and under this category we managed to get three features on to regional television. Each item bore some evangelistic witness. There are also great opportunities on those local phone-in programmes. When working on one such programme I was thrilled to hear a Christian caller with something relevant to say.

Television, radio and newspapers use up vast quantities of material every day. Those who have the gift of putting scripts, stories and programme outlines together should never be afraid of submitting their ideas. Most of us get more refusal notes than commendations, but there's no harm in trying! After all, Christians in Britain are an important minority group, and it's only fair that our beliefs should be adequately reflected in the local and national media.

*   *   *

Through these and other experiments in evangelism our teams have come to understand that only the Holy Spirit produces lasting results. Success achieved in our own strength is short-lived. In countless ways we have known the Lord's guiding, providing and chastening hand. Not all our experiences have been easy or fruitful, and sometimes there has been real opposition and sheer despondency. On the whole, however, the use of the media in dozens of different missions has been a rewarding and exciting experience — perhaps never more so than when, on one memorable occasion in a Spanish bar, the gospel went into five different languages simultaneously as the Roadshow proceeded. It seemed like the start of another Pentecost! Come to think of it, perhaps Pentecost had something to do with learning to speak the language of the people.

Some useful addresses

Street Theatre: Training is given by FOOTPRINTS THEATRE COMPANY who will visit your area to lead workshops and present their own productions. Write to:

FOOTPRINTS THEATRE COMPANY, Hillcrest, 128 Oldham Road, Grasscroft, Oldham, Lancs.

Films: For a full list of films and addresses see chapter ten.

Music: Groups suited to your situation and needs will be recommended by:

BRITISH YOUTH FOR CHRIST, 52-54 Lichfield Street, Wolverhampton WV1 1HW.

Gospel Roadshows: Addresses and suggestions will be supplied by:

The Rev. Rob Frost, 15 Denham Crescent, Mitcham, Surrey CR4 4LZ.

A full script entitled 'The Travelling Salvation Roadshow' together with production notes and music is available from:

REFLECTION, 26 Eastbourne Avenue, Acton, London W3 6JN.

Mass media: Courses in communication skills are provided by:

CHURCHES TV AND RADIO CENTRE, Hillside, Merry Hill Road, Bushey, Watford WD2 1DR.

5 Cliff College Missions

ROBERT A. MASON

Director of Evangelism at Cliff College

The aim of Cliff College missions has always been two-fold: to support local churches in the priority task of bringing people to Christ, and to provide practical training in evangelism for the Cliff students. To these ends the college maintains a full-time staff of four evangelists, recruited from among students who have completed the one-year basic course and a further year of specialisation in evangelism. The evangelists hold missions throughout Great Britain and Ireland, always at the request of local churches or Christian groups.

There are two basic types of Cliff mission:
1. **Evangelists' Missions** which take place at any time of the year during term time and last usually for 10-16 day periods. The normal team is of 2-4 members.
2. **Students' Missions** which are led by evangelists or college tutors with a larger team of 8-10 students. Two or three such teams can be combined to work in a group of churches or even a whole Circuit. There are three periods of student mission:
   A long weekend in November
   Ten days in early spring ending on Palm Sunday
   Three weeks in the summer beginning the last week in June.

There is no specific method distinctive to Cliff evangelism. It is normal to arrange a variety of events giving evangelistic opportunity in and around the local church which has invited the team. Preaching rallies, more or less traditional, still form an important part of any mission though they are much less frequent than formerly. Pedestrian shopping areas in many towns make an ideal site for modern open-air preaching. The old style of soap-box preacher plus a group of hymn-singers has given way to the use of sketch-boards. The speaker stands, usually alone, and teaches the message of salvation as he builds up simple line-drawings on his board. The success of this technique is remarkable both in gathering a group of listeners and in bringing people actually to the point of decision. We owe our adoption of this type of outreach to the Open Air Campaigners (27 Southdown Avenue, Brighton, West Sussex BN1 6EH) whose yearly visit to the college forms part of the course in evangelism.

Whenever requested to do so our teams are glad to work amongst children in order to strengthen an existing Sunday School or to establish a new one. The old stand-by of Cliff missions, the Sunshine Corner, has gradually been transmuted into an Adventure Club, but although the name has changed the format of games, quizzes, choruses and stories is timeless. The appeal of such meetings is as great as ever it was in many areas.

Of the less traditional methods used, the most important are House Groups, school visits and drama. During a typical mission at least a couple of evenings will be spent with discussion groups of 8-10 people meeting in a home. One or two students or evangelists will lead the group, talking about aspects of the Christian faith and sharing their own experience of Christ. Flexibility in the content and style of these meetings, as well as the close personal contact possible, is an obvious advantage of this kind of approach.

All our attempts at reaching young people today involve visiting schools. There is at present a remarkable willingness on the part of teachers and school authorities to accede to requests by evangelists to visit their schools. The aim in so doing is not precisely to preach, but rather to testify to an experience of Christ. A normal school assembly would contain a song, a personal testimony, a simple sketch illustrating some aspect of the gospel and a 'publicity spot' for the mission. The emphasis on personal experience suits the prevailing trend in RE towards 'living religion', and Cliff students often have the added appeal of not being too much older than the senior pupils themselves. Through schools work it is possible to make contact with virtually all the teenagers in the area, and to invite them to such things as Christian Coffee Bars arranged for their age-group in the evenings.

A television age needs to see as well as to hear the gospel. Evangelism through drama is designed to meet this need. Presentations vary widely from a few simple sketches, dramatized parables, to reasonably elaborate Roadshows which are virtually musical plays. Comedy has been found a powerful tool in the service of the gospel. An extension of Cliff's open-air work that is being increasingly used is street theatre, often simple mime with a narrator. This soon attracts a crowd and affords yet another opportunity to make the gospel known.

The use of any or all of these various methods

depends as far as possible on the particular objectives of the local church and the special needs of the area. Whatever the local variations, however, the fundamentals remain the same: to offer Christ as Saviour and Lord, both to those who do not know him at all and to those whose knowledge of him is only slight.

It is difficult to state correctly and concisely the impact a Cliff mission has. There are around fifty each year, and there are probably as many opinions of their impact as there are missions. A questionnaire is sent to all church leaders for their assessment following the summer Student Missions, and responses vary enormously from unqualified praise to undisguised disappointment. Quotes from 1978, for instance, include both 'They made a tremendous impact' and 'Some church folk see hardly any benefit for all the expense'. Most churches state the number of decisions for Christ registered as an indication of the degree of success. Missions where there are no open decisions are in the minority, but signed Decision Cards say nothing of the permanent results of this type of evangelism. Probably the major problem confronting us is the inability of so many local churches to provide adequately for the spiritual needs of those who make an open response during a mission. Permanent impact depends as much on the follow-up of the host church as on the Cliff team itself.

A general impression from reports is that the numbers who make a first-time decision for Christ are largely drawn from the age-group slightly younger than the students themselves — middle and late teens. Typical comments from recent reports have been: 'A work has begun . . . especially among our young people'; 'The lady members of the team gave a lot of time to our teenage Club girls with very real signs of them coming through to full commitment'; and '50% of the Youth Fellowship accepted Christ'. Another consistent impression gained is of the general quickening of the pulse-rate of churches after a mission. This is often put down to the enthusiasm and personal influence of students and evangelists. Quoting again from our most recent reports: 'The team's enthusiasm and love were the chief influence'; 'The week of mission led by Cliff College students has left us richer and blessed'; and 'The team had evident joy and ability to share their joy in the Lord'.

Specific areas of renewal in church life following a mission include a heightened awareness of the need for evangelism, and a new desire for deeper spirituality through prayer and Bible study. This is strongly evidenced by the frequent wish to continue some aspect of the mission's activity after the departure of the team. Often the Housegroup idea survives in the form of a regular fellowship. One or two Circuits have continued holding rallies on a monthly basis, for evangelism or the deepening of the spiritual life of members. We regularly see numbers of young people attending the Cliff Anniversary and Derwent Convention who have turned to Christ during a Cliff mission. Not a few Cliff students give as their main reason for applying to the college the influence of students and evangelists during a mission in their area.

An important advantage, especially of Evangelists' Missions, is the opportunity to look at a church in a way that it cannot easily look at itself — objectively.

Very often a visiting team can challenge a church more pointedly, and without causing offence, than local leaders and preachers. Student Missions have the benefit of larger teams, and so a wider range of talents. Cliff preaching always contains a note of personal experience, and this emphasis has an appeal in an age when experience is valued and theory is suspect. The practice of students and evangelists being accommodated in homes gives them opportunity to show the gospel in behaviour as well as to proclaim it in words. We constantly receive testimony in letters to the way faith and love have been communicated by a student's stay in a home.

The brevity of even the longest missions is a disadvantage. The duration of Student Missions is determined by the college calendar and is inflexible. Evangelists' Missions could be extended, but rarely are because of traditions about the length of special missions and also because of questions of finance. We are seeking to offset this handicap by encouraging churches to see a Cliff mission as only one part of a much longer programme of renewal. To this end we hope soon to be able to recommend a specific programme to be used by the host church before and after the mission, and to supply literature for it.

The expenses incurred in a Cliff mission vary considerably. The overall cost is influenced by factors such as travelling distance from the college, incidental travel costs during the mission, quantity and quality of publicity materials and the use of ancillary services such as Christian film agencies. The average cost of a ten-day summer mission with a team of 8-10 students is currently £150-£200. No charge is made for students' services, but a gift for the work of the college is usually given.

There are three situations in which a Cliff mission could prove particularly useful:

1. Where a short period of direct challenge to decision is felt to be needed. This is often the case when a considerable amount of 'pre-evangelism' has been undertaken, resulting in a number of adherents who have no personal experience of Christ.

2. Where a hard or untouched area is seen to be potentially fruitful but the active church membership is limited. This calls for a lot of hard work, visiting, informing the community of the existence of the church and sharing the gospel with individuals. It is not recommended, however, when the church's limitations are spiritual (in the area of faith and prayer) rather than physical (in the area of age and numbers).

3. Where growth in a specific church department is seen to be necessary and feasible in terms of available local manpower. In this way Sunday Schools, Youth Groups or regular Family Services have been started or developed through a Cliff mission.

It is worth repeating that the essential usefulness of most Cliff missions is as part of a continuous programme of renewal which sees evangelism as an integral part of the church's regular activity. Where it is regarded as an event which happens every few years at the instigation of a handful in the congregation who are 'inclined that way', or as a means of importing a team to do the church's evangelistic work for it, a Cliff mission is unlikely to have any lasting impact.

For further details

More information about Cliff missions and future dates for which teams are available may be obtained from:

The Director of Evangelism, CLIFF COLLEGE, Calver, Sheffield S30 1XG.

6 One Step Forward

PETER GOOD

Minister of Whiteabbey Methodist Church, Newtownabbey, Northern Ireland

'Yes, we have decided to use *One Step Forward* in Rwanda and Burundi.' I was with Bryan Gilbert in the offices of the Danish Baptist Union in Copenhagen as the General Secretary made this announcement. Now *One Step Forward* was to be used in the work of mission and evangelism in Africa!

One Step Forward (OSF) materials have been made available to hundreds of churches in some thirty countries in Europe (East and West), America, Australia, Brazil and Argentina. Rumanian Christians can listen to the whole OSF concept on radio as it is beamed from Monte Carlo, and materials have been translated into many languages. But what is the OSF concept? It is best described as a Bible-based programme for local church growth through commitment, training and evangelism. It requires no outside expertise (except for the use of the OSF literature described below), and can be adapted to suit any local church situation.

The founder and International Director of OSF, the Rev. Bryan Gilbert, trained at the Royal Academy of Music and went into show business before answering the call to the ministry. During the nine years he spent as a Baptist minister in England he conceived the idea of a pattern for continuous local church evangelism, and called it 'One Step Forward'.

Other ministers and churches became interested, and in 1966 he had to make the choice between remaining as the pastor of one church and making himself available to serve many churches. He decided on the latter, and now spends his time explaining the concept of OSF to other ministers, Methodists among them, in this country and abroad.

There are four parts to the OSF programme, and ideally it takes one year to complete. As the name *One Step Forward* suggests, each stage of the programme builds upon the previous stage as follows:

Part One: OPERATION AGAPE

Using a 12-week study book (ideally every church member should have a copy), help is given with human relationships within the church fellowship. It also makes people aware of the needs of others. There are five basic ideas which are followed through at this first stage, based on the letters of the Greek word *Agape* (love):

Avoid criticism and gossip daily

Go and visit someone in need weekly

Another acquaintance each month

Pray daily for others

Encourage someone each day

Part Two: SPIRITUAL GROWTH AND COMMITMENT

By use of a four-week study book (again, ideally all who attend church regularly should have a copy), help is given in drawing the 'fringe members' to commitment to Christ, in deepening the spiritual life of all believers, and in mobilising them into action. On the fourth Sunday at the morning service, everyone is challenged to make a Covenant, indicating on a card provided their commitment, their rededication or the offering of their time in some practical form of Christian service.

Part Three: INSTRUCTION IN EVANGELISM

The workbook for this part provides 11 studies for Growth Groups on various aspects of evangelism. The approach mixes teaching and theory with practical opportunity. A copy of the workbook should be available for all who attend the Growth Groups.

Part Four: EXPRESSION EVANGELISM

This final stage includes both social concern and evangelistic outreach. It is a time for the whole church, using all its varied gifts, to tell the neighbourhood the message of Jesus.

*   *   *

Way back in 1974 I was discussing with my church leaders plans for some sort of mission during the Year of Evangelism which was to be in 1975. I am minister of Whiteabbey Methodist Church situated in Newtownabbey, six miles to the north of Belfast on the shores of Belfast Lough, and with 250 families claiming membership. But then I heard about *One Step Forward,* one of a number of schemes for lay training in evangelism listed on a duplicated sheet sent out by the Methodist Home Mission Division in London. I wrote for more information and interested my leaders in the idea. Eventually, instead of a traditional style mission, we launched out on an OSF Campaign which began in September 1974 and went on until June 1975.

'Operation Agape' made an immediate impact on the life of our church. The work of evangelism was advanced as members set their minds on the New Testament teaching about 'agape', Christian love. I preached sermons on the theme during the twelve weeks of this first stage. Part Two (Spiritual Growth and Commitment) brought visible evidence of the Holy Spirit at work in our midst. On the fourth Sunday, sixty people returned their Covenant Card indicating commitment to Christ, renewal of commitment or offering help in a variety of ways from visitation work to supplying flowers for Sunday services. This was to be a turning point in the spiritual life of our church.

Part Three followed (Instruction in Evangelism). We could have wished for more of our people to be involved in these studies, but those who did attend the Growth Groups grew in Christian maturity and some are now actively involved in the work of Lay Witness Missions.

Expression Evangelism (Part Four) is ongoing and open ended. We do not claim to be the perfect church! Attempts to motivate people into action always seem to present problems. We set up an active Community Service Committee, however, and its work continues. But the most important result was, and continues to be, the new ability of a number of our people to share their faith. We have more than twenty people, young, middle-aged and old, who can speak about their commitment to Christ. Teams go out to take mid-week meetings and Sunday Services in other churches.

I have no hesitation in commending *One Step Forward.* The programme can be tailored to suit different local situations, but note that it is important to take leaders and key workers with you in planning.

From my own experience, Parts One and Two are much less difficult to implement than the later stages which may present problems in getting people interested and ready to risk moving forward. With prayer, planning and perseverance, however, good things will result. If the complete programme is thought to be impossible in your church, Part One could be attempted on its own, perhaps then moving on later to tackle Part Two.

OSF materials are reasonably priced. Complete sets are available for £2. The study book for Part One costs 20p, Part Two 15p and Part Three 20p. Posters and cassettes are also available. So the campaign will cost money. If we were to start all over again in our church it would cost us about £100 at today's prices. But *One Step Forward* has proved of extreme value. It has been used by the Holy Spirit to change many lives and churches. That was its intent, and that is what it is still accomplishing not only in our church but in others where the OSF programme has been used. Our experience in Whiteabbey is interestingly echoed by that of the Rev. Maurice Jelbert, Superintendent of the Hemel Hempstead and Berkhamsted Circuit in England, who has summed up OSF's value in this way:

'The programme of OSF has come as a breath of fresh air — surely the wind of the Spirit — to me and the people of my Circuit. Five churches are finding much blessing through it. There are certain emphases of this Bible-based and practical programme which should appeal to us as Methodists:

1. The stimulus to the study and practice of Christian love as found in the New Testament and emphasised by John Wesley.

2. The encouragement to meet together for prayer and Bible study.

3. The importance given to the place of personal Christian witness in word and action.

4. The thrilling opportunities for preachers to share in team preaching.

The Lord is using this movement in many countries and churches. I pray that its great help may be known by 'the people called Methodists' in fellowship and service'. Why not consider it in your church?

For further information

Write to the following address for details, OSF materials or to request a visit to your church:

ONE STEP FORWARD, High House, 13 Lutterworth Road, Walcote, Leicester LE17 4JW.

Bryan Gilbert and his associate, David Greenaway, are prepared to travel anywhere in Great Britain to speak about their work and explain further the planning of an OSF campaign.

7 Lay Witness Missions

COLIN R. NOWELL

Minister of the Blackburn Central Mission

'Sunday morning's service brought me into a full conversion to the Christian faith. Up to that point I thought I was a Christian in the full sense; but after being in the midst of people I had never met, and the warmth and love and friendliness they had, I realised that Jesus Christ could mean so much more in my life. On Sunday morning I responded fully and willingly to Christ's call. Now I know that each step I take, I take with Jesus Christ. My family has been united with Jesus. We are now complete. In our home we have begun to read the Bible together, followed by a prayer. I know that this is just the beginning and that each day will bring all our family a step nearer to Christ.'

That particular Sunday morning service was the climax of a Lay Witness Mission held at Bamber Bridge Methodist Church near Preston, and the testimony is typical of many which have resulted from similar missions held up and down the country over the past two years. The Lay Witness Mission movement was started in America by the Rev. Ben Johnson, and has spread rapidly to many parts of the world. In the United Kingdom it is promoted and co-ordinated by the Institute of Church Renewal whose headquarters are in Bolsover, near Chesterfield, and missions in this country are now staffed entirely by Christians from our own British churches.

Sometimes called 'a caring and sharing weekend', a Lay Witness Mission is a weekend event designed primarily to awaken the nominal Christian to a personal faith in Christ. A group of Christians drawn from different churches and backgrounds, and led by a co-ordinator appointed by the Institute of Church Renewal, is invited to a local church for a carefully planned weekend to share their faith with those who attend. This sharing is the central feature of the mission, for whilst other types of evangelism concentrate on the public proclamation of the gospel, the approach of the Lay Witnesses is rather to speak personally on a one-to-one basis or in small groups about their experience of Christ. The sharing which takes place .is a two-way process, however, and frequently team members return home feeling that they have received as much as they have given.

Whilst the weekend programme may vary slightly from one situation to another, the following sequence of events has proved itself a good basic outline:

Friday

5.00-5.30 pm	Team members arrive.
5.30-6.00 pm	Team meeting.
6.00-7.00 pm	Church Family Supper followed by singing and sharing by two or three of the visitors.
7.30-9.00 pm	Sharing in small groups under the leadership of team members. Questions such as 'What would you like to see happening in your church this weekend?' and 'What would you like to see happen in your own life this weekend?' are discussed together.
9.00-9.30 pm	Reporting back.

Saturday

9.00 am — Team meeting.

10.30 am — Coffee Groups in members' homes to share about and explore prayer.

12 noon — Lunch. The men and women (and sometimes young people) of the church often meet for lunch separately to share their particular concerns.

6.30 pm — Church Supper followed by further sharing in small groups. There is no reporting back this time, but the church is open for prayer at the end of the evening.

Sunday

9.00 am — Team meeting.

11.00 am — Morning Worship during which the co-ordinator shares his testimony and invites members of the congregation to join him at the communion rail to make or renew their commitment to Jesus Christ.

2.00 pm — Team members leave for home.

6.30 pm — Evening Worship. After an opening time of worship the church evaluates the weekend as members are invited to share what it has meant for them and discuss where the church should go from here.

One of the first British churches to hold a Lay Witness Mission was Lammack Methodist Church in Blackburn, and the story of that experience is told in the booklet *New Lives for Old* (available from the Institute of Church Renewal). In it, the Rev. Robert

Teasdale writes: 'What did the Lay Witness Mission do for Lammack? It brought the church alive in a new way, in the right way. Many of the forty or more people responding to the appeal on the Sunday morning were leaders of the church making a deeper surrender of their lives to Christ. Twelve of those who answered the appeal were not members of the church, but we expect to receive some of them into membership in April. The church is different. There is a new feeling of love, a new concern for the things of the faith, for the community and for individual people. Our membership at Lammack when we started this was 74. By April we expect it to be nearly 100.'

When a church reaches the stage of considering seriously the possibility of holding a Lay Witness Mission, the first step is to contact the ICR (Institute of Church Renewal) who will arrange for a representative to visit the church and explain what would be involved. If the decision is taken to go ahead, an application form is completed giving details of the church, and the ICR begins to consider prayerfully the appointment of a co-ordinator. The co-ordinator will usually make two visits before the mission in order to help the church in its preparation, for which a detailed Preparation Manual is available. Experience has shown that a close adherence to this helps to ensure that the church receives the maximum benefit from the weekend.

The co-ordinator and all the team members give their services to the church without cost, and travel at their own expense. However, the church is responsible for providing them with hospitality over the weekend, and the number of team members is generally reckoned on the ratio of one to every eight or ten church members expected to attend the mission. In addition to the hospitality, the church is responsible for the cost of publicity, printing and the church family meals.

The impact of a Lay Witness Mission will vary according to those who decide to share in the weekend. These will include those who are right at the heart of the church's life and some on the fringe who accept invitations to come to the Church Suppers and Coffee Groups. Almost inevitably there will be some who stay away — often wishing afterwards that they hadn't! It is in essence a mission *to* the church rather than a mission *from* the church to the complete outsider. In this sense it is a proven method of 'pre-evangelism'. Those who 'come alive' spiritually during the weekend become keen to share their faith with others and often become team members on missions elsewhere. Some, too, become Local Preachers or find other ways of sharing their new-found faith in Christ.

For further details

Write to the INSTITUTE FOR CHURCH RENEWAL, 37 High Street, Bolsover, Chesterfield, Derbyshire.

8 Celebrating the Faith

BRIAN R. HOARE

New Testament Tutor at Cliff College

The past few years have seen the development in many parts of the country of interdenominational town-wide missions, often characterised by a 'festival' atmosphere. Such events in places as diverse as Newcastle, Plymouth, Manchester, Peterborough and Cheltenham have drawn large numbers of people. Even more ambitious was the 1978 Mission to Cornwall which sought to involve people in many different parts of the county. Similar 'festivals' are already being planned in a number of other parts of Britain.

What is the thinking behind this type of 'celebration evangelism'? Christians have always recognised the importance of the occasional large gathering, but have been slow to see its real potential. For decades in Methodism the Circuit Rally was a feature of Circuit life, sadly now on the wane in many areas. Events like 'Come Together' in recent years, and more established gatherings like the Keswick Convention and the Cliff College Anniversary weekend, have proved their worth in bringing the people of God together in large numbers. Yet the Old Testament Jews could teach us a thing or two about how to celebrate our faith together! Events like the Feast of Tabernacles and the Feast of Unleavened Bread, with all the excitement of trumpets, water ceremonies, giant candelabra, torchlight processions, and crowds of up to three million singing pilgrims, must have been impressive indeed.

In his analysis of the factors that characterize a growing church, Peter Wagner has suggested the following formula:

Celebration + congregation + cell = church

Whilst many of our congregations have exploited the 'cell principle' through housegroups and small fellowship meetings, we have largely neglected the importance of the sort of 'celebration' which is only possible when large numbers of Christians gather together for worship. Quite apart from the benefit of such gatherings to Christians themselves, their evangelistic potential is considerable, and it is this that we consider more fully here.

One of those who has pioneered 'celebration evangelism' in Britain has been David Watson, vicar of a large and lively Anglican church in York. On most of his missions he has been accompanied by a team of his own church members who have specialized in developing the use of music and drama in the service of the gospel. Others who have been used to lead this type of town-wide evangelism have included the former Bishop of Coventry, Cuthbert Bardsley (who led the Cheltenham 'Festival of Faith') and the former Principal of Cliff College, Howard Belben (who led a recent 'Mission to Peterborough'). What have been some of the features of these and similar missions?

First, they have always been *interdenominational.* It is probably true to say that in the early days of such missions the initiative came largely from evangelicals. The Leeds Christian Festival entitled 'The Whole Story' began, for instance, with an idea developed by the evangelical Anglican church, St George's, and was carried through by a committee of like-minded Baptists, Free Evangelicals, Brethren and a Methodist. Sometimes, as in the case of the 'Mission to Peterborough', the venture has been the outcome of planning by the local Council of Churches. More often, however, it seems to have been the result of a few enthusiastic Christian leaders in a locality getting together more informally to share their concern and vision for their town. Latterly, such ventures have drawn support from a much wider theological and denominational spectrum — often a reflection of the way in which the Renewal Movement has been used to break down the barriers that have for too long existed between fellow believers. In Cheltenham, for instance, the Roman Catholics agreed to hold their own parallel mission, and actually joined in both the opening and closing meetings in large numbers. The working party planning a fortnight of united mission in Southport includes two Roman Catholic priests. The task of celebrating and proclaiming the gospel is coming increasingly to be seen as one which overrides our church divisions.

A second feature of this type of evangelism is that it employs a wider *variety of activities,* and thus gives expression to a wider variety of gifts, than the more narrowly conceived type of mission. The scope is almost unlimited. In addition to the main evening meetings there may be such things as lunchtime talks or gospel concerts, Christian films, street theatre, open air services, dancing, flower festivals, exhibitions of Christian art, bookstalls, missionary exhibitions, street questionnaires, an enquiry shop or caravan, children's painting or hymn-writing competitions, schools' activities, student events — and almost anything else that any individual, group or church felt able to contribute to the whole. The Leeds festival featured an enormous bookstall of Christian literature in the largest covered shopping precinct in the city; the *Yorkshire Post* and the Trustee Savings Bank allowed TEAR Fund and Christian Aid exhibitions respectively on their premises; and craftwork from the Third World was on sale in the Merrion Centre. The 'Festival of Faith' programme in Cheltenham included such diverse musical talents as a Methodist choir, a Salvation Army gospel group and a Baptist group of interpretative dancers. The bigger the venture, the more variety can be afforded in the hope that those who are not attracted by one approach will be reached by another.

Thirdly, it becomes obvious that events planned on this sort of scale can be so much *more ambitious.* For one thing, a greater financial income is guaranteed. A budget of even several thousand pounds can be covered relatively easily when so many groups and churches are actively involved in support. Top films can be shown, singers of national standing can be engaged, and publicity can be extensive and of a high quality. The brochures and posters at one festival were of such a high standard that even professional advertising men were known to enquire who had done them! A further spin-off of an ambitious programme is that it is more likely to attract the interest and coverage of the media. The local press, radio and even TV have been found extremely co-operative when presented with the sort of activities that have really caught their imagination — and this has all provided valuable extra free publicity.

Fourthly, perhaps the main outcome of a Christian festival is that *Christians themselves are encouraged.* What Howard Snyder has written of the great city-wide gatherings which have become a regular feature of church life in Sao Paulo, Brazil could equally well apply to the British situation: 'Tomorrow they will be scattered in hundreds of congregations around the city, many of which are small and struggling. But they will not be discouraged. They know that they are part of a people, a movement!' Or, as one lady wrote from Cheltenham: 'The whole festival was glorious! It was so encouraging to actually meet together with so many of the Christians in the town.' That in itself is all to the good, for Christians whose confidence in the gospel is increased because they have celebrated their faith with hundreds of fellow-believers are much more likely to be outgoing in further evangelism than those whose horizons are never extended beyond their own small and struggling fellowship.

But fifthly, the actual *evangelistic impact* of such festivals is not insignificant. There will always be those within the churches who need to be brought from mere church allegiance to personal commitment to Christ. As the Rev. William Gowland has put it, 'The church is not only a force for mission, but a field for mission'. It has been the common experience of most of the festivals we have mentioned that the majority of those who have been led to Christ have already had at least tenuous church links. But they were by no means all who were reached by this type of evangelism. The Rev. Jeffrey Sharp, a Methodist minister involved with 'The Whole Story' in Leeds, reported: 'I know that during the week the Lord moved many from outside the normal church circle to come in and see for themselves'. The 'big event' drawing large crowds and with a multiplicity of activities has a snowball effect, and people can come and go out of mere curiosity without any feeling of obligation or identification. For some, indeed, curiosity has proved the first step on the road to faith.

We have assumed here that 'celebrating the faith' is something that can only really be done in cities and towns where there is a large population and a good number of churches to support the event. It is worth noting, however, that similar events have been success-fully organised in rural areas. The 'Mission to Cornwall' was a case in point, covering as it did not only the larger towns but some much smaller communities also. Some years ago now, as reported in the *Epworth Review* by the Rev. David Sharp, a project called 'The Jesus Way' was arranged with the dual aim of training Christian young people and reaching out to other young folk in rural North Derbyshire. Here too, the method used was that of bringing people together in an atmosphere of joyful Christian celebration. With the exception of Derby itself, all the other centres used were small country towns: Chesterfield, Bakewell, Matlock, and Alfreton. Whilst the approach in rural areas will obviously have to be somewhat modified and adapted, therefore, 'celebration evangelism' is by no means to be seen as a method applicable only to large urban communities.

For a last word, what better than a comment from David Watson: 'There is today a new, joyful purpose springing up within the church. Christians from all backgrounds are joining hands together in Christ, are being released into new areas of praise and worship, and are working together for a positive proclamation of God's good news.' And so it should be. Perhaps someone in your area might catch the vision?

For further information

Those who are thinking of organising events of the sort we have described and who would like to be put in touch with others who have already had the experience of what is involved are invited to write for names and addresses to:

Dr Clifford Hill (Secretary for Evangelism and Church Growth), EVANGELICAL ALLIANCE, 19 Draycott Place, London SW3 2SJ.

A comprehensive report of the Cornwall Mission and the way it was planned is available (50p post free) from:

The Rev. Charles Sibthorpe, Dove House, Agar Road, Truro TR1 1JU.

9 Saying it with Music

JOHN WEBSTER

*Minister in the Ryedale Circuit
of North Yorkshire*

The ex-Benedictine nun and Irish pop singer, Maureen O'Hara, has a song that says 'music speaks louder than words'. Although this is only a half-truth, there is a great deal of sense in what she says. Many people have become impervious to words, especially the words of a preacher, but it has been known ever since the time David played for King Saul that music not only has a calming and relaxing effect but also puts the listener in a more receptive frame of mind.

The mid-seventies saw the advent of *Come Together,* a musical written by two Californians, Carol and Jimmy Owens. Described as 'a musical experience of Christian love', it has had an enormous impact upon both worship and evangelism in many parts of the world. Indeed, it may be questioned whether anything, apart from the Billy Graham Crusades of a former decade, has proved quite as effective an evangelistic tool. Experience in the Manchester area convinced me that here was a way to open the hearts of many people, both young and old, who might not respond to other methods of evangelism. Especially memorable was a night at the Queens Hall in Wigan when, after a performance of *Come Together* by a local choir, an appeal was made and between fifty and sixty people came forward for counselling.

How could we transfer this idiom to the local church? We tried a local shortened version of *Come Together,* but the complex modern music did not seem to lend itself easily to the church situation. Why not therefore put together our own programme of simple songs selected from the spate of hymns and choruses written in recent years, and weave them into a theme?

Moving to the rural Ryedale Circuit in North Yorkshire I found a number of talented people interested in music and singing who agreed to co-operate in the experiment. Since scripture instructs us to sing a new song (Psalms 96:1, 149:1), why not obey this command and develop the theme? Our first programme was thus entitled *Sing a New Song,* and aimed both to introduce folk to some of the new Christian music and to remind them that even the old favourite Methodist hymns (like those of Moody and Sankey and the Salvation Army) were once new too.

Using music and songs from *Sound of Living Waters, Fresh Sounds* and *Come Together,* as well as a number of scripture verses set to music, we presented an evening of praise and introduced many to worship and prayer in the medium of song. As in *Come Together,* there was a time to move about and share fellowship with others present. The evening also included a short evangelistic address and an opportunity for people to respond to the message. A duplicated copy of the words was given to each member of the congregation, and all were encouraged to join in with the choir when they felt they had begun to know the tune. We felt very strongly that the purpose of the choir was not to perform to the people, but to teach and lead the gathering in praise

61

and worship. The inclusion of an old hymn from the Sankey collection known to most of those present was appreciated, and was not felt to be at all out of place.

Much encouraged by the very favourable response to our first effort, and urged on by the Circuit Ministries Committee, we began to prepare another presentation. This time it was perhaps a little more ambitious and much more evangelistic in outlook. The title *Life Abundant, Life Eternal* was chosen and practising began. We sought to show how Jesus Christ imparts abundant and eternal life through his word, through his body and blood and through union with himself. A song entitled 'Born again . . . you can be born again' (from the sequel to *Come Together* called *The Witness,* also by Carol and Jimmy Owens) became our theme song, and proved very effective evangelistically in preceding and following the presentation of the gospel message. The minister of the large church in which we put on the first presentation said in his welcome that he had never seen the church so full of people for a worship service — except at the funeral of a local dignitary! Some time later we were invited to a smaller chapel in the nearby market town of Malton. On that occasion not only was every seat taken and a very warm and receptive atmosphere created, but we know of at least one person whose life was given to Christ that evening. It is worth noting also that, in addition to the evangelistic impact of these evenings, the twenty or so members of the choir were greatly blessed through the times of fellowship they enjoyed both in preparation and performance.

Seeing the tremendous potential of this kind of evening, appealing as it does to all the family, we perceived that the same approach might be used for teaching doctrine to the church whilst at the same time continuing to present an evangelistic message. Since we had recently been discussing in the Circuit how each church member might become more effective and how we might improve local pastoral oversight, the theme *You are the Body of Christ* seemed an obvious choice.

You are the Body of Christ began with scripture being read by a number of voices, and also gave our musicians an opportunity to let the music speak for itself without words. The programme allowed time for the congregation not only to move around and get to know one another, but also to form small groups to pray for specific needs. It concluded with a simple communion service, the elements being distributed to the people by a number of stewards. Remembering that John Wesley believed Holy Communion to be 'a converting ordinance', we felt that to receive the body and blood of Christ was the most symbolic way of all to receive Jesus into one's life — even more meaningful than raising a hand in a meeting or coming to stand at the front. We therefore invited those who loved Jesus (that being the only restriction to the table) to receive him into their lives as they took the bread and the wine.

The preface to the *Methodist Hymn Book* begins with the words 'Methodism was born in song'. We have come to believe that if she is to be reborn we must pay attention to the music that is given to the church by inspiration of the Holy Spirit, and encourage people to 'sing a new song' as they did in the days of the Evangelical Awakening. For music is not only the outcome and expression of faith in

Christ; for some it can become the very means whereby they come to know him.

Some conclusions

1. When the initial hesitancy is overcome it has been found that people enjoy being involved in singing. Although at first very reluctant to move about in the church and greet others, once they began to do it we had great difficulty in getting them together again to continue the programme!

2. It is relatively simple to select a theme and choose hymns and choruses to fit in with it. Alternatively one can take a number of songs that particularly appeal and weave a theme around them. Either way no special musical or literary expertise is required.

3. The benefit of fellowship and the experience of working together for those who prepare for the presentation is worth while in itself. In our case it was not possible to get the whole choir together at one time, so a cassette recording was made of the music thus enabling small groups and individuals to practise without all coming together.

4. We have sought to encourage anyone with any kind of talent to use and develop it in the service of the Lord. One lady made large banners for display in the churches with words such as 'Rejoice in the Lord always' and a matching banner for the other side of the church saying 'Again I say rejoice'. Others were 'We are the body of Christ' and 'We are one in Christ Jesus'. On another occasion a group of ladies was invited to decorate the church with flowers, using the theme of the presentation as titles for their arrangements.

5. We have been especially encouraged to see all age groups taking part and working together in harmony. We now have some younger children wanting to join with us and play tambourines and other percussion instruments. On two occasions some of the younger members of the choir have interpreted the songs in simple dance steps, with the addition of coloured ribbons to express the joy and gladness of the occasion.

6. We have felt that making known the presentations by widespread advertising has helped to encourage a good attendance. Leaflets were home-produced, once again using home-grown talents in art and design.

Some useful music sources

Besides the better known hymn books, the following will be found useful as sources for many of the more contemporary songs and choruses:

Scripture in Song, A collection of 205 songs published by Anchor Recordings, 72 The Street, Kennington, Ashford, Kent.

Sound of Living Waters and *Fresh Sounds,* compiled by Betty Pulkingham and Jeanne Harper (Hodder and Stoughton).

The Singing Word, A songbook produced by Youth With A Mission and published by Truth Press International, D-8931 Hurlach, West Germany.

Psalm Praise, A sequel to the well-known *Youth Praise* books containing a varied selection of psalm paraphrases set to new music (Falcon Press).

10 Film Evangelism

TREVOR JACKSON

*North-East Regional Officer for the
Centre for Television and Radio Communication*

Have you ever considered the amount of time the
average viewer spends watching television in one week
or even a month? Taking only 3½ hours viewing a
day, which is below average for the winter months,
we arrive at a ratio of one day in seven, but by
computing these figures several stages further it totals
a staggering ten years in one lifetime.

What has this to do with film evangelism? Since we
are thinking about communication and the way in
which opinions and attitudes are shaped, it is worth
observing that many young people would far sooner
argue that something was true because they 'saw it on
television', than because they had 'read it in a book'.
Every day, programmes are broadcast with the object
of entertaining or educating us, and yet the use of
visual-aids for presenting Christian truth within our
Churches is so very often neglected.

There are many channels open to us for obtaining
16 mm. films to use in evangelistic outreach and to
assist the ongoing work of teaching and motivating
those within our Churches. Several film titles and
useful sources are outlined in this chapter to help you
make a start, or perhaps extend any work you have
already undertaken in this field.

In many areas there is an increasing awareness of
the valuable part film can play. In Yorkshire alone

there are twelve Methodist Circuits involved in using the Lord Rank Film Scheme, with many other Circuits affiliated to it. The idea of this approach to evangelism is that where there may be a group of Churches, irrespective of their denomination, who are keen to utilise a set of 16 mm. projection equipment and/or a selection of films on a fairly regular basis, the Centre for Television and Radio Communication (CTVC) through its various Regional Officers can offer advice and assistance. Write for more details of the Film Scheme and the costs involved to: CTVC, Walton Road, Bushey, Watford WD2 2JF.

At Knaresborough, the Head of Religious Education at the King James's School is using films in the classroom on certain days and then, according to their suitability, in Churches around the Circuit at week-ends and on some evenings. The venture is proving to be very worth while and a valuable lead-in to discussing issues relating to the Christian faith. In the Hawes Circuit, which is largely rural, some of the smaller societies have been using films in the context of worship, and a local farmer who is working closely with young people finds that having a projector in the Circuit offers several opportunities for hiring films to sustain a work of outreach.

The success of any film presentation hinges very much upon the kind of preparation that has been put into it, and this we can examine by looking at

PREPARATION — SOME DO'S AND DON'TS

DO think about the purpose behind your film showing. It is important that your aims are clear from the beginning. It is often worth remembering that a film can be used in a situation where perhaps the 'preacher' would not be so acceptable. You will need to decide on

    (a) *The length and type of film* you want — Christian challenge or testimony style, a discussion starter or documentary?

    (b) *the best venue* for showing it.

    (c) *whom to invite* and your approach to publicising the event. The Christian Publicity Organisation assist many churches in this field. Write for information to: CPO, Ivy Arch Road, Worthing BN14 8BU.

    (d) additional points such as a competent projectionist, a bookstall and/or free literature to cater for follow-up afterwards.

DON'T put on a film without either previewing it first or accepting the judgement of someone who has seen it. From time to time film previews are arranged by CTVC in different parts of the country, and any available information on them can be sent if you write for details.

Some film libraries may be willing to lend films for previewing purposes only. You would need to be well organised in terms of having a good number who would like to see them before explaining your situation and offering one or two dates. After all it would amount to free publicity for them.

DO plan your film or series of films at least two-three months ahead where possible. When writing to various libraries for catalogues, hire charge details, etc., ask about discounts. You may discover that in booking a film for several days there are useful savings to be made. If you are planning to present two or three films in one evening there are several sources for obtaining 'free loan' films. These can often provide a good introduction to the main film and for a relatively small handling charge can be very useful.

RECOMMENDED FILMS
FOR EVANGELISTIC AND
TEACHING PURPOSES

Outlined below are a number of films which can be used effectively in a variety of situations. The film title, running time, hire charge and source are given, along with a recommended age group. All the sources listed offer catalogues or literature on additional films and in some cases they make a charge for supplying this.

WHERE THE WATERS RUN 28 mins. £7 (FF) 13 +

Exploring the uniqueness, amazing properties and value of water upon which we are totally dependent for life. It presents the similarities of natural water to the 'water of life'. Useful for schools and youth groups but suitable enough for older groups.

THE CAGED 55 mins. £10 (EFF) 15-20 years

An Anglo-Dutch production. The story of two young people, Benny and Anneke, who are torn apart by her drug habit. Amidst all the problems they encounter, Anneke becomes a Christian and Benny reflects at the close on the change that she has experienced. Good for teenage groups. Evangelistic.

TROUBLED WATERS 40 mins. £9 (EFF) 18-25 years

Filmed on and around the Colorado River this adventure on an army raft brings out lessons on guidance and Christian discipleship. Plenty of action, showing young people facing life in the raw. Good for

69

older teenagers and in conjunction with another film.

HIDDEN ISLAND 35 mins. £6.50 (EFF) 8-13 years

This evangelistic children's film provides a beautiful setting of sporting action with a clear presentation on becoming a Christian.

FIESTA 30 mins. £7.50 (CF) 14+

A modern version of the 'prodigal son' parable. Excellent for use with teenagers upwards.

CHRISTMAS IS 18 mins. £4 (CF) 6+

A cartoon style production. Popular with all ages. A refreshing approach to the Christmas story. Ideal for Sunday Schools, family worship, etc.

CELEBRATION NOW 12 mins. £4 (CF) 13-18 years

One of a series of three titles. Fast moving, suitable for coffee bar work or in conjuction with a longer film.

BIG SPLASH 30 mins. £6.50 (LL) 8-12 years

A film designed to teach important values to children, with most of the action centring around a swimming competition.

YONEKO 45 mins. (LL and EFF) 15+

The true story of an 18-year-old Japanese girl who tried to take her life as a result of depression, loneliness and doubt. While in hospital Yoneko receives a visit from Christians who share love and hope with her. Suitable for Christian Unions and Youth groups. Evangelistic/Christian Challenge.

THE GOSPEL ROAD 67 mins. £15 (WW) 15+

Based on stories from St John's Gospel, Johnny Cash has blended songs and music together in order to provide a beautiful interpretation of the life of Christ. A very popular film for evangelism with most age groups.

DEVIL AT THE WHEEL 40 mins. £10 (CTVC)
15-30 years

A teenage rebel from a well-to-do family becomes engrossed in a life of crime. A surprising chain of events brings about a change of direction for him. A true story re-enacted by the teenager concerned makes this a fascinating testimony film.

FOLLOW ME 32 mins. £7 (CTVC) 15 +

An encouraging, yet challenging film about Christian discipleship. Portraying the Mitchel family who decide to put their faith to the test in day-to-day relationships at home and work. Christian challenge/discussion starter.

OH HAPPY DAY 11 mins. £5 (CTVC) 14 +

One of many shorter films obtainable from this source, it portrays Jesus in the guise of a street sweeper, meeting a variety of people who respond by following him everywhere. Although without dialogue the film is easy to follow and would provide an excellent discussion starter on the claims of Christ.

MARTIN THE COBBLER 26 mins. £7 (CTVC) 7 +

Based on the story 'Where Love Is, God Is' by Tolstoy. This animated film using clay models with remarkable effect portrays an old Russian cobbler whose life is not what it should be because he lives only for himself. Excellent for all age groups especially Sunday School, family worship context.

ONE MAN'S PARISH 23 mins. £5 (CTVC) 14 +

A Yorkshire Television production featuring Rev. Rob Frost and his work as a Methodist Minister. Useful for lead-in to discussion on methods of evangelism with Sunday School teachers, leaders, etc. Potentially useful in a worship context also.

71

A WARLORD MEETS CHRIST 30 mins. £7 (CTVC) 14 +

An excellent film featuring a United States Air Force pilot, Heath Bottomly, who tells his own story of the way Christ transformed his life. Suitable for schools and youth clubs/married couples.

WHERE JESUS WALKED 27 mins. £6 (CTVC) 14 +

Produced by Classic Television Films of Israel this superb production uses Bible passages. The narrator brings a refreshing approach to the gospel story. Suitable for mid-week fellowship meetings, Bible study groups and wider audiences.

ZOONOOZ 20 mins. £5 (CTVC & LL) 7 +

Filmed and interviewed at a Zoo in Australia, George Cansdale compares the habits of animals in relation to humans. The animals are beautifully filmed and the simple message will appeal to all ages. Excellent for children/family worship.

An outline of feature length films available in 16 mm.

THE CROSS AND THE SWITCHBLADE	105 mins. £30 +	(NFC)
MOSES	141 mins. £25	(CTVC)
THE TEN COMMANDMENTS	222 mins. £30	(RF)
BROTHER SUN AND SISTER MOON (St Francis of Assisi)	122 mins. £18	(RF)
JESUS CHRIST SUPERSTAR	107 mins. £35	(RF)
THE BIBLE . . . IN THE BEGINNING	157 mins. £16	(FDA)
THE ROBE	134 mins. £16	(FDA)
BARABBAS	139 mins. £12.50	(CWD)

GODSPELL 110 mins. £25 (CWD)

All the above films are available in colour. All prices quoted usually represent ONE showing of the film and *do not include* additional items such as postage (some libraries use Securicor or British Rail), insurance, VAT and publicity where this is available. You may need to add an additional £2-£3 *at least* to cover your costs.

Film Source Guide

CF   CONCORDIA FILMS, Viking Way, Bar Hill Village, Cambridge CB3 8EL. Tel. 0954-81011

CTVC CTVC, Foundation House, Walton Road, Bushey, Watford WD2 2JF. Tel. 0923 35444

CWD   COLUMBIA-EMI-WARNER DISTRIBUTORS LTD., 135 Wardour Street, London W1V 4AP. Tel: 01-439 7621

EFF   EVANGELICAL FILM FELLOWSHIP, 67 Linnet Drive, Chelmsford, Essex CM2 8AG. Tel. Chelmsford (0245) 59475

FDA   FILM DISTRIBUTORS ASSOCIATED (16 mm.) LTD., Building No. 9, GEC Estate, East Lane, Wembley, Middlesex HA9 7QB. Tel. 01-908 2366

FF   FACT AND FAITH FILMS, 37 Coton Road, Nuneaton, Warwickshire CV11 5TW. Tel. Nuneaton (0682) 381690

LL   LIGHT AND LIFE FILMS, 42 Fountainhall Road, Edinburgh EH9 2LW. Tel. 031-667 1607
      or
      4 Pandora Street, Donegall Road, Belfast BT12 5PR. Tel. 0232 41550

NFC   NATIONAL FILM CRUSADE, PO Box 4, 179 Whiteladies Road, Bristol BS99 7SA. Tel. 0272 312817

RF   RANK FILM LIBRARY, Rank Audio Visual Ltd., PO Box 70, Great West Road, Brentford, Middlesex TW8 9HR. Tel. 01-568 9222

WW   WORLD WIDE FILMS, Shirley House, 27 Camden Road, London NW1 9LN. Tel. 01-267 0065

Additional sources of 16 mm. films

BRITISH AND FOREIGN BIBLE SOCIETY, AVA Dept., 146 Victoria Street, London EC4V 4BX. Tel. 01-248 4751.

CONCORD FILMS, 201 Felixstowe Road, Ipswich, Suffolk IP3 9BJ. Tel. 0473 76012.

INTERNATIONAL FILMS, 235 Shaftesbury Avenue, London WC2H 8EL. Tel. 01-836 2254

YOUTH FOR CHRIST SERVICES, 52-54 Lichfield Street, Wolverhampton WV1 1DG. Tel. 0902 771063

Sources of 16 mm. films available on free loan

GOLDEN FILMS, Stewart House, 23 Frances Road, Windsor, Berks. SL4 3AF. Tel. 07535 69566

BP FILM LIBRARY, 15 Beaconsfield Road, London NW10 2LE. Tel. 01-451 1129

RANDOM FILM LIBRARY, 25 The Burroughs, Hendon, London NW4 4AT.

TRANSPORT & TRAVEL FILM LIBRARY, Melbury House, Melbury Terrace, London NW1 6LP. Tel. 01-262 3232

11 Using Christian Literature

STEPHEN ENGLISH

Scripture Union evangelist
and
PHILIP AND MARY PECK
Local Preachers in the Rugby and Daventry Circuit

Never have our Christian bookshops been so full of good reading. Rows of dull, colourless books are things of the past, and even the most conservative of publishers go to great lengths to present their wares attractively. Yet the fact remains that if people do not buy and read them, their message is wasted. The Lord's command to go into all the world and preach the gospel surely includes the enthusiastic use of Christian books. Our purpose here, therefore, is to explore some of the ways open to us, and to share our experience of what we have seen accomplished through Christian literature.

The church bookstall

Certainly no church should be without its bookstall! It brings a sense of vitality, a feeling that the church is alive and concerned. It provides a helpful focal point at the close of a service, and visitors and new arrivals can often be contacted more readily as they browse around the display of books.

The bookstall has many benefits to offer a church. First, there is the benefit to church members themselves. Good Christian books can feed and stimulate, can challenge and deepen the devotional life, and can give us a fuller understanding of our faith. Secondly, a well chosen book can have a profound effect on the uncommitted or nearly convinced fringe member. It will almost certainly have to be lent or given, but can provide a valuable talking point as we later enquire 'What did you think of it?' For the definite non-Christian friend, sceptical or just indifferent, books can again prove a most useful tool as we seek to defend or offer the faith that is in us.

The church bookstall, however, must be run well. Its effectiveness or otherwise is largely due to the people responsible for it, and they need to keep up to date with new books, find time to read them themselves, or keep abreast of the book reviews. Knowledge and enthusiasm are basic requirements for the job. Knowledge of the right books for the right occasion, and the enthusiasm to set out the stall well using display stands and other attractive advertising aids. Skill with a felt tip pen can be an invaluable asset!

The following practical suggestions may be of help to those considering setting up a church bookstall for the first time:

1. Consult the Church Council and seek official approval for the project. Questions such as where it is to be sited, when it is to be open, what equipment will be needed and who is to pay for the initial outlay will all need to be faced early on.

2. Approach the nearest Christian bookshop to discuss supply facilities. The manager may be willing to supply books on a straightforward 'Sale or return' basis, but no discount is usually granted on such transactions. The best arrangement is to set up as a

Book Agent with the shop. If the manager agrees, the appropriate Publishers' Association form has to be completed (available from the bookshop or from the Publishers' Association, 19 Bedford Square, London WC1), and he can then allow you a 10% discount on all books which can go into church funds or be used to buy more literature for outreach work. It should be noted that a Book Agent can only deal with the shop at which he is registered, cannot sell stock below the normal price, and must sell at least £50 worth of books a year. That may seem a large target, but you will be surprised at how easily it is reached. A turnover of several hundred pounds a year is by no means uncommon for a church bookstall.

3. Once the Book Agency has been agreed, further questions will have to be decided. Will stock be supplied on 'Sale or return'? Will the shop insist that what you take you have to keep? Could a monthly change of books be arranged to prevent the display from becoming dull and over-familiar?

4. Next, the content of the bookstall has to be decided upon. With hundreds of titles to choose from it can be a daunting task indeed! Don't be shy about asking for help. The manager will know the best selling paperbacks of the month; children's books are a must; Bibles in their many versions will probably need to be included also; Christian comics are popular with the youngsters. Birthday cards, bookmarks, pens and pencils all add to the interest and variety. Make it known that you are eager to offer a service, and will obtain books not in stock. Keep a simple stock sheet so that you know what

you have without rummaging through endless boxes under the table.

5. Be on the lookout for special opportunities for the bookstall. The approach of Christmas is an obvious one, and stock can be built up with gift books in mind. The Church Anniversary or Missionary Weekend afford further opportunities, especially if the visiting preacher is an author whose books can be prominently featured. Special weeks of mission will bring new faces and the reappearance of lapsed members, and here too is a field for evangelism through literature.

A book 'First Aid' box

This is another idea for literature evangelism, more particularly for use as a tool in personal evangelism. The idea is to build up some ten or twelve paperbacks to keep as a kind of spiritual 'First Aid' for people with problems. There may be a bereavement, or someone taken ill; we may come across someone with a particular query about the Christian faith, or someone really seeking to know more about the Christian way of life. How important it is to have a suitable book on hand . . . 'Here, read this. It helped me a lot. We'll talk about it later on'. The book may not have all the answers, but an opening has been made. Keep your books up to date, then, and pray that they will be used.

Book parties

In an age when many of our neighbours are holding parties to sell kitchenware, cosmetics, even under-wear, why not hold a book party? These can be held almost anywhere, and over the past few years we have known them in churches, schoolrooms, village halls, Playgroups, Young Wives' Groups, and all manner of private homes in both town and village. The most worthwhile, however, have usually been found to be those held in a home, arranged perhaps by just one couple who have seen the opportunity and been prepared to put their house at the Lord's disposal. One young mum, for instance, invited about twenty of her friends to a 'Coffee Morning Book Party' and sold over £50 worth of books. Quite simple invitations were penned on the back of old Christmas card pictures. Toddlers were welcome, and a simple crèche operated in one room while coffee, chatting and selling went on in another.

Or come to a little village near Bicester. Here the Wesleyan Reform Church hold an annual Book Party in their schoolroom. Over the past three years sales have averaged £100; but even more important than the amount of money taken is the fact that the majority of folk who have come along are non-churchgoers who are beginning to discover the value of Christian books. Contacts are made and personal conversations ensue. Problems have come to light, and counsel and prayer can be offered.

On a larger scale still, a succession of 'Book-Ins' was arranged in Rugby. On the Friday, the curate of a church in a neighbouring town held a stall for his parishioners in his home during the morning. Friday evening was devoted to the parents of the local Crusader Class (with some of the senior boys and girls helping). A Saturday Coffee Morning and Book Market at the Circuit Methodist Church in the centre of the town (with posters advertising it outside the church) was followed with a repeat at an evening Fellowship Meeting at the same venue. Obviously such a project can be adapted to suit a wide variety of

79

local conditions, but it wants no more than the will to set about it and a clear idea of aims. If you have a church bookstall from which to draw stock, so much the better. If not, most Christian bookshops will be glad to co-operate, for the Book Party is an extension of their own ministry and is an idea alive with opportunities.

Finally, let us consider briefly some of the many other ideas for spreading the gospel by means of literature:

1. An evening 'Book Bonanza' might be included in the church's midweek programme (perhaps a joint meeting of the housegroups), at which the local Christian bookshop manager can talk about the ministry of Christian literature and suggest further ways in which the church might make use of it.

2. It is well worth applying for Christian books through the local public library. If they have to obtain new copies, they then go on their shelves for others to see. Many who would not otherwise have any contact with Christian books may well take and read them.

3. In some churches it is possible to hold a bookstall on the church forecourt. This obviously depends on local circumstances, and is probably best used on high days and holidays only, but it has been tried with encouraging results.

4. Writing in *Span* (the magazine of the London City Mission) David Linley tells of a Christian bookstall he started with his wife's help on Hoxton Market in 1975. It is open every Friday, and both new and second-hand books are stocked. Local people will linger and talk, there are opportunities with the 'regulars' who stop to chat, and contacts are made

with people from all over the world. Market stalls like this need to be regular, and require a degree of dedication that is not easy to find. But once relationships have been built up over the weeks and months they can prove a most fruitful field for personal evangelism.

5. Local Agricultural Shows and Trade Fairs present a good opportunity for a Christian bookstall, as on a larger scale do County Shows. Expense will be involved in the renting of the site and stalls, and there will be fierce competition to gain the attention of the passing public. Church displays and bookstalls therefore have to match up to the high standard of the surrounding exhibits, and those who man them need to be well informed.

*   *   *

Although most churches are within easy reach of a Christian bookshop, there are still areas which lack this facility. Perhaps they may be encouraged by the story of one small house fellowship meeting in an outlying estate of the town. Its members had the vision of what might be accomplished through a Christian bookshop, and although only about fifteen strong they stepped out in faith. They were eventually led to shop premises very close to the centre of the town, and in particular close to the open market held on Fridays, Saturdays and Mondays when all the surrounding district come in to the local cattle market.

The venture started six years ago with no more than £200 worth of books on the shelves. Both the shop and a full-time worker were supported by the fellowship, until after about three years it became a going concern. Today it has become a source of Christian literature for a wide area, and there have been conversions through its ministry. It stands as a wonderful example of what the Lord can do through the faith of a few and with limited human resources — but loaves and fishes indeed!

For your church newsletter

We have not dealt in this chapter with the possibilities for literature evangelism through local church newsletters, but the opportunities are real. The following agencies offer a regular supply service of material which can be adapted and used to suit your local needs:

RELEASE NATIONWIDE, 142 Dantzic Street, Manchester M4 4DN

> Well-written, professionally edited and presented short articles aimed at the man in the street who doesn't have much time for church.

EVANGELICAL NEWS SERVICE, 127 Suez Road, Cambridge CB1 3QD

> Short news items, articles, topical features and quotes aimed more at the churchgoer than the complete outsider.

Both agencies will send sample packs on request.

12 **Personal Evangelism**

HOWARD A. G. BELBEN

Former Principal of Cliff College

There are three ways in which Christians may witness for Christ: by what they are, by what they do and by what they say. Most Christians recognize the importance of the first two, but fight shy of the third.

Sometimes people have a fantasy of a personal evangelist as a pushing personality bulldozing a defenceless stranger with an aggressive 'Are you saved?' We do well to substitute for this Daniel Niles' definition: 'One beggar telling another beggar where to find bread.' By personal evangelism we mean simply the one-to-one sharing of Christian faith and experience with someone who does not yet know Christ.

Church Growth experts say not more than 10% of church members show any special gifts as evangelists. It would be easy for the rest to say, 'I'm one of the 90%, so I'll settle for making my witness with my life.' But from the New Testament church onwards personal evangelism has not been limited to those with much education, training or outstanding gifts. Much of it was done by ordinary Christians who had a tongue in their head, and judged that the most important discovery of their lives was a suitable topic of conversation. It still is.

HOW DO I SET ABOUT IT?
Here are twelve pieces of advice.

1. Be prepared. We can prepare by getting to know

what we believe better than we do now. We need to read, learn, think and talk with other Christians about our faith.

2. **Be prayerful.** God knows which are the prepared hearts, and we need to keep tuned to his wavelength. Personal evangelism is not human salesmanship. It is possible only through the work of the Holy Spirit in both parties.

3. **Be alert.** Openings often come unexpectedly, and can easily catch us on the wrong foot, so that the moment passes and the opportunity is missed.

4. **Be friendly.** An act of will is needed to overcome our natural reserve. Most people warm to genuine friendliness, personal interest in them, and thoughtful, neighbourly acts.

5. **Be natural.** There is no need to be embarrassed. We can learn to be as natural and relaxed as a child is when he talks about God.

6. **Be relevant.** Find a point of contact with the interests of one you are trying to win. You watch the same television and have the same concern about world and national problems. Show the relevance of Christ to modern man in his frustration, aimlessness, restlessness, emptiness, loneliness, but offer also abundant life in Christ to man in his strength.

7. **Be simple.** The offer of the gospel is not complicated, or some would be excluded. It is easy to be side-tracked into arguments on side-issues, but people are seldom argued into becoming Christians.

8. **Be Bible-based.** Many personal evangelists take a New Testament, or at least a gospel, with them wherever they go. Do not throw texts at people in any automatic way, but have at your fingertips

some of the great verses that have brought thousands to Christ, such as John 1:12; 3:16; Romans 3:23 with 6:23; Revelation 3:20.

9. **Be personal.** Be ready to give your own testimony to the difference Christ has made in your life. Avoid giving an impression of moral or spiritual superiority. Be honest about your own weaknesses and focus attention on what Christ has done for you.

10. **Be Christ-centred.** Our aim is not just to persuade people to come to church, or to adopt Christian values: it is to introduce them to a Lord and Saviour who died for them and offers to live in them now by the Holy Spirit.

11. **Be definite.** People tend to postpone a response to the gospel. They prefer vague discussions. Do not rush them, but when you believe they have understood what it means to be a Christian and have faced the cost of discipleship, be on the watch for the moment when you can lovingly confront them with the need for a decisive response of faith. If they say they would like to accept Christ, pray a simple prayer, then encourage, but do not press them, to pray aloud also. Then the vital follow-up work begins.

12. **Be expectant.** See non-Christians, even the worst, as they might be. Believe that what God has done for you he can do for them.

CAN PERSONAL EVANGELISM BE ORGANIZED IN A CHURCH?

No Christian need wait for anyone's permission before becoming a personal evangelist. In one sense it cannot be organized, but a church can do three things to encourage and assist it:

1. **It can provide training for those who are prepared to witness.** Through fellowship meetings as well as Sunday preaching, the church can provide four things that contribute to the training of personal evangelists: (a) a deepening understanding of people (b) a knowledge of basic Christian doctrine, (c) familiarity with key texts of Scripture that sum up the heart of the gospel and (d) some basic Christian apologetics, such as will help our people to give a reason for the hope that is in them. Preachers will do well to review the range of their subjects and class leaders their programmes, to see whether they are providing for these needs.

2. **It can encourage Christians to be articulate about their faith.** Christians are unlikely to engage in verbal witness to an unbeliever if they have never before put their own beliefs and experience into words. We can give them the opportunity to do this by (a) providing small sharing groups, similar to the old Methodist class meetings, and held generally in the relaxed atmosphere of a home, and (b) providing them with opportunities to give their testimony publicly at a Sunday service, a women's meeting, a youth fellowship or an open-air meeting. Some may welcome an invitation to write down their testimony and show it to their minister or leader.

3. **It can arrange a specific training programme.** This may be a short sandwich course of instruction coupled with a chance to engage in personal witness through house-to-house visitation or visitation from prepared lists of fringe contacts. We have too readily assumed that such visiting will have the important but limited objectives of offering

those visited the help of the church or inviting them to special services. But there is growing evidence that definite personal evangelism is possible in people's homes, if visitors go prepared to share their faith and, if the way opens, to point people to Christ after having established a relationship with them.

WHAT HELPS ARE AVAILABLE?

1. Training materials

A number of evangelical organizations produce training materials and aids for use in personal evangelism. Methodists who have used some of these have at certain points found themselves questioning some of the teaching and methods suggested, but an immense amount of experience has gone into their producton and there is a great deal to learn from such organizations as the following:

CAMPUS CRUSADE FOR CHRIST, 105 London Road, Reading RG1 5BY.

CRUSADE FOR WORLD REVIVAL, Box 11, Walton-on-Thames, Surrey.

THE FISHERS' FELLOWSHIP, 96 Plaistow Lane, Bromley, Kent.

EVANGELISM EXPLOSION, 11 Saint Denys Road, Portswood, Southampton.

THE NAVIGATORS, 27 High Street, New Malden, KT3 4BY.

ONE STEP FORWARD, High House, Main Road, Walcote, Lutterworth, Lciccster LE17 4JW.

OPERATION MOBILISATION, 142 Dantzic Street, Manchester, M4 4DN.

2. Study programmes

There are two, both produced by the evangelical

Anglican organization called the Church Pastoral Aid Society, which have been found of help in some Methodist churches after slight adaptation:

Warren, Norman, *Signposts* (Falcon Booklets). A training programme for use with a group of people committed to personal evangelism.

Parish Evangelism devised by Gordon Jones. A more comprehensive study programme dealing with personal evangelism as a basis for the church's outreach, and comprising books, filmstrips and recorded talks. Available from Falcon AVA, Falcon Court, 32 Fleet Street, London EC4Y 1DB.

3. Books on personal evangelism

Three of the most useful books are the following:

Little, Paul E., *How to give away your faith* (Inter-Varsity Press). This is written largely for Christian students, in a racy, often amusing, American style. The first six chapters in particular are full of practical, down-to-earth advice. It includes useful sections on basic questions we may be asked and on the relevance of Christ today.

Pawson, H. Cecil, *Personal Evangelism* (Saint Andrew's Press). A moving plea for one-to-one evangelism by a man of wide experience in it. It contains many useful ideas expressed in telling ways.

Pilkington, Ross, *Lifestyle Evangelism* (Scripture Union). Written for groups learning together how to share the love of God in continuing relationships. It is clear, practical, stimulating and generally convincing.

4. Booklets

Many booklets have been written on the subject. The best of these give a great deal of practical guidance in a short compass. Those listed below complement one another, and it is worth reading all of them and absorbing their contents.

MacInnes, D. R., *An Introduction to Personal Evangelism* (Falcon Booklets).

Wood, Maurice A. P., Bishop of Norwich, *How can I lead someone to Christ?* (Islington Booklets No. 7, Scripture Union).

Stott, John R. W., *Personal Evangelism* (Inter-Varsity Press Booklet).

Thompson, D. P., *Personal Work for Christ* (St Ninian's Centre, Crieff).

Postscript: Planning for Growth

GEOFFREY JONES

Minister of South Chadderton Methodist Church, Oldham

Early on in my ministry as a layman, a group called the Navigators demonstrated to me the essential importance of personal evangelism: concentrating on one person, leading him to Christ and teaching him 'to teach others also', as Paul instructs young Timothy. I believe the basic unit in evangelism to be the individual Christian, and whatever is not based on that unit is unrealistic. It is for this reason that I have sought regularly to preach clear gospel messages, calling for response and offering both personal counselling and such practical help as is given in booklets like *Journey into Life* (Falcon Press) and *Becoming a Christian* (Inter-Varsity Press). We have prayed specifically for people to be converted; we have gathered those who showed real interest into a home to study the Bible; we have built up monthly Family Services, Supper Clubs, Family Nights and Houseparties so as to extend our 'catchment area' for evangelism; and we have held a 'mission to the church' using an evangelist who realized that his brief was mainly to seek to bring nominal church members to a living, personal faith. All this has been done with the aim of building up a church made up of members who have a real experience of Christ, and who are able to share their faith with others. Without that, all our 'methods of mission' are rendered null and void.

The need, however, is not merely to obtain decisions, but to make disciples. The small cell in which believers can be built up has proved invaluable in subsequent evangelistic work. Here they have learned God's word, how to witness to others, and how actually to lead another person to faith in Christ. It is a vital basis for solid spiritual growth.

As the number of committed Christians has increased they have been encouraged to take up work in the church and to move into positions of leadership. From the growth of committed individual Christians we have moved on to plan for the growth of a whole church entirely geared for mission. This requires long-term planning, and one must not be impatient. Real growth always takes time. Bringing forth a baby is a mere nine month process, but real maturity takes 20, 30, 40 years. We have prayed and planned, therefore, to make the Church Council more spiritually and evangelistically minded. We have sought to break down the formality of our church committees, and to make them into fellowship groups which pray together and spend time discussing how the concerns for which they are responsible can be used in the total outreach of the church. We have sought to develop 'mission consciousness' at every level of church life, and firmly but lovingly to insist on the evangelistic policy the church has adopted. We have shared our vision with the Circuit staff, with the Circuit Meeting and with the Local Preachers' Meeting, and thus been able to develop special Guest Services, theme preaching, visits from teams from Christian colleges, and the wider use of our own gifted church members.

The church's evangelistic policy has been worked

out in many different ways, using many of the methods described elsewhere in this booklet. We have a major evangelistic campaign about every two years, with a visiting evangelist to lead us. Experience has convinced us that this must be both a culmination of careful work over that period of time and a springboard for future work. The visiting evangelist needs to be brought in very early on in the planning, so that his own personal approach and the church's evangelistic policy can be compared and aligned.

We have held regular children's missions to back up the teaching being given in Sunday School and midweek groups. In our case we have used both Children's Christian Crusade (23 Waltham Road, Manchester M16 8PG) and Open Air Campaigners (27 Southdown Avenue, Brighton, West Sussex), and all planning, preparation, training, counselling and follow-up work has been in close co-operation with their staff workers.

With young people we have concentrated on building up leaders' groups and weekly fellowships, and have tried to ensure that the leadership of the Youth Club, Brigades and Covenanters is in the hands of mature and committed Christians. At monthly intervals we take them into the open air for personal work combined with singing and illustrated talks, and involve as many of them as possible in both planning and carrying out this act of witness. Saturday mornings outside the market hall, evenings on the streets and Sunday nights during the summer outside the Town Hall have proved to be perhaps the most fruitful form of direct evangelism we have. As we have gone out where the people are, we have found many to be really interested in what we have had to say.

Other evangelistic work we have attempted has included specially prepared musical sessions using modern methods and drama. When backed by careful preparation, high standards, imaginative publicity and individual effort to bring friends and neighbours, these have made a significant impact. We have engaged in visitation using the *Challenge* newspaper (published by Challenge Literature Fellowship, Revenue Buildings, Chapel Road, Worthing), a Christian tabloid in *Daily Mirror* format which concentrates on presenting the gospel through human interest stories as well as straight information about medical matters, cars, gardening and so on. We have involved ourselves in bigger events such as the Manchester Festival led by David Watson, and this too has added new Christians to our church. It proved also to be a most valuable way of stimulating training in evangelism and follow-up, providing a 'well' of Christians equipped and ready to share their faith with others.

So the church grew. Our members trebled in five years. Yet in my personal search for a co-ordinated approach to evangelism I became frustrated when the next three years brought only a 'plateau' in our growth. I knew that God wanted more, yet my mind constantly rationalized the guilt I felt at having been given so much and only being able to maintain the *status quo*. Christian friends reassured me by saying 'Quality matters more than quantity . . . Consolidation is the thing . . . Spreading love among Christians and showing it to the community is our true vocation'. I grasped these half-truths readily, for

93

they eased the burden of the Great Commission of Jesus constantly to extend God's kingdom. Yet the frustration remained in the light of the facts.

It is only recently that I have found that the insights of the Church Growth movement present that sort of comprehensive way of looking at the ongoing life and work of the local church for which I had been searching. As we have begun to study its principles and implement them, sometimes involving us in agonising and prayerful reappraisal of the church's life and my own ministry, we have been stimulated to a new faith-expectancy for the future and have discovered new guidelines for growth in the present. In particular, the effects of considering and acting upon the following ideas have been far-reaching in their helpfulness:

1. For evangelism to bring consistent growth the church must function as a healthy body

Four areas are involved here:
  i. Growing up (in knowledge of Christ)
 ii. Growing together (in love and fellowship)
iii. Growing more (new Christians)
 iv. Growing out (in influence in the area)

Diagnosis in all these areas is vital. In which areas have we declined? What positive growth factors do we possess? We have set up working parties whose brief is to assess each of these fields of ministry and to suggest goals and plans for the next five years. Our aim is then to bring all those plans together, and over the next six months to set specific targets for the church. These we will present to the membership, amend as necessary and then pursue as one body with a clear vision of our life and work together.

2. Spiritual gifts in the body must be discovered, offered and utilised

Using Lewis Misselbrook's pamphlet *Discovering Spiritual Gifts* and the Bible Society's workbook, we are encouraging everyone in our fellowship groups to find out (and to help each other to find out) just what gifts God has given them which might be used to help the whole church to function as he wants it to. All manner of gifts are coming to light and the variety and richness of our church life is bound to be greatly enhanced.

3. Both minister and church must be prepared to change, and to pay the price that growth will involve

A radical self-analysis of one's own ministry is quite a challenge! Do I *want* to change? Do I really believe in continuous growth? Can I take the disturbance involved? Above a public blood-pressure testing machine was the caption: 'What you don't know about yourself could kill you'. But when you *do* know it you almost die of shock!

With the background of Church Growth insights the church too can be helped to assess itself in this way. Its level of expectation can be raised, and some of those practical factors which have hindered real growth (not just 'Your faith is not great enough' or 'Your dedication is faulty') can be uncovered. Those that are capable of change can be changed, and those that are not can at least be better understood and more intelligently taken into account in our future planning.

What sort of changes might be found necessary? It may be that a change of overall aim in the church is needed so that evangelism is made a primary goal in every part of its life. More is required of us than simply to keep the church efficiently ticking over. It may be that we shall see the need for setting specific 'faith goals', or for a more serious effort to undergird our church life with believing prayer. Perhaps we need to develop the sort of enabling structures, cell groups, of which we have spoken earlier. Certainly we shall need to do all we can to ensure that our worship is lively and inspiring, recognizing this to be a common characteristic of all growth situations.

The Church Growth principles are certainly not the only way of 'planning for growth' in the local church, but they do provide the best way I have found of looking comprehensively at the church with a view to a consistent policy of continuing spiritual increase. I believe that churches in Methodism can and will grow in these coming years. We Christians are in the growth business, constantly seeking increase both in our quality of life and in the numbers of those who possess and live that life through Christ. Where growth happens, however, it is almost always because someone has had the vision and belief that the church *can* and *will* grow, and has offered himself wholly to God to enable it to happen. May those who read this booklet be counted among their number.

Some helpful literature on Church Growth

Harris, Jeffrey, *A simple introduction to Church Growth* (Methodist Home Mission leaflet).
Thomson, Robin, *Can British Churches Grow?* (BMMF, 352 Kennington Road, London SE11 4LF). A workbook comprising nine units of study for personal or group use. A valuable practical introduction to the whole subject.

McGavran, Donald, *Understanding Church Growth* (Eerdmans).

Information on other Church Growth literature will be supplied by:

CHURCH GROWTH BOOK CLUB, EMA, 19 Draycott Place, London SW3 2SJ.